中国思想文化术语多语种对外翻译
标准化建设项目成果

CHINESE THINKING AND CULTURE
MULTILINGUAL TERMINOLOGY DATABASE

中华源·河南故事
CHINESE CIVILIZATION
Stories from Henan

青铜器

BRONZE TREASURES

河南省人民政府外事办公室　编

·郑州·

图书在版编目（CIP）数据

中华源·河南故事. 青铜器 / 河南省人民政府外事办公室编. -- 郑州：河南大学出版社，2022.11
 ISBN 978-7-5649-5350-8

Ⅰ. ①中… Ⅱ. ①河… Ⅲ. ①地方文化－河南－通俗读物②青铜器（考古）－河南－通俗读物 Ⅳ. ① G127.61-49 ② K876.41-49

中国版本图书馆 CIP 数据核字（2022）第 217606 号

青铜器
QINGTONGQI

责任编辑	任湘蕊
责任校对	屈琳玉
封面设计	翟淼淼
版式设计	高枫叶
出版发行	河南大学出版社
	地址：郑州市郑东新区商务外环中华大厦2401号　邮编：450046
	电话：0371-86059701（营销部）
	0371-86059750（高等教育与职业教育分公司）
	网址：hupress.henu.edu.cn
排　版	河南大学出版社设计排版部
印　刷	河南博雅彩印有限公司
版　次	2022年11月第1版　　印　次　2022年11月第1次印刷
开　本	710 mm×1010 mm　1/16　印　张　12.25
字　数	200 千字　　　　　　　定　价　62.00元

版权所有，侵权必究
本书如有印装质量问题，请与河南大学出版社营销部联系调换。

"中华源·河南故事"系列丛书编委会

顾　　问	黄友义	杨　平	范大祺		
主　　任	梁杰一				
副 主 任	卞　科	陈　岩	陈志伟	刁玉华	方启雄	韩国河
	惠　康	焦开举	介晓磊	孔留安	李冰冰	李　俊
	刘炯天	李向前	李　镇	梁留科	刘金锋	马萧林
	牛书成	牛卫国	屈凌波	屈鹏飞	史永庆	田　凯
	万正峰	王建修	王清义	王自文	许二平	杨建伟
	杨玮斌	俞海洛	张改平	张俊峰	张明超	张松文
	赵卫东					

主　　编	梁杰一					
副 主 编	李冰冰					
编　　委	陈国良	陈　玮	丁　锐	高　阳	徐恒振	郑延保
	孙立英	郭　远				

中华源·河南故事·青铜器

主　　编	马萧林
副 主 编	李　琴　钱建成
中文撰稿	李　琴　张俊儒　刘丁辉
英文译者	王志伟　穆念伟　李文竞
英文审校	[美] Jason Anthony Aldous

The Editorial Committee
Chinese Civilization
Stories from Henan

Consultants	Huang Youyi　Yang Ping　Fan Daqi
Director	Liang Jieyi
Deputy Directors	Bian Ke　Chen Yan　Chen Zhiwei　Diao Yuhua
	Fang Qixiong　Han Guohe　Hui Kang　Jiao Kaiju
	Jie Xiaolei　Kong Liu'an　Li Bingbing　Li Jun
	Liu Jiongtian　Li Xiangqian　Li Zhen　Liang Liuke
	Liu Jinfeng　Ma Xiaolin　Niu Shucheng　Niu Weiguo
	Qu Lingbo　Qu Pengfei　Shi Yongqing　Tian Kai
	Wan Zhengfeng　Wang Jianxiu　Wang Qingyi　Wang Ziwen
	Xu Erping　Yang Jianwei　Yang Weibin　Yu Hailuo
	Zhang Gaiping　Zhang Junfeng　Zhang Mingchao
	Zhang Songwen　Zhao Weidong
Chief Editor	Liang Jieyi
Deputy Chief Editor	Li Bingbing
Editors	Chen Guoliang　Chen Wei　Ding Rui　Gao Yang
	Xu Hengzhen　Zheng Yanbao　Sun Liying　Guo Yuan

Chinese Civilization
Stories from Henan
Bronze Treasures

Editor-in-Chief	Ma Xiaolin
Associate Editors-in-Chief	Li Qin　Qian Jiancheng
Writers	Li Qin　Zhang Junru　Liu Dinghui
Translators	Wang Zhiwei　Mu Nianwei　Li Wenjing
Translation Proofreader	Jason Anthony Aldous (U. S.)

总　序

中国是世界四大文明古国之一，也是世界上唯一的古代文明传统未曾中断的国家。河南省地处中国中东部，是中华文明和中华民族的重要发祥地，在中国五千年的文明史上，河南作为国家政治、经济、文化的中心就长达三千多年。从某种意义上讲，一部河南史就是半部中国史。这里是中华人文始祖黄帝的故乡，是古丝绸之路的东方起点，是少林功夫和陈氏太极的发源地，这里创建了中国历史上最早的都城，镌刻了中国最古老的文字，诞生了中国最初的商业文明。

伴随着新时代的荣光，河南经济社会发展迅速，人民生活水平显著提升，这是河南人民自力更生、艰苦奋斗的历史结果，也是对外开放带来的益处。河南经济社会的发展、人民生活方式的改变都植根于深层次的文化积淀。为了让世界更多地了解河南，让河南更好地走向世界，2018年以来，河南省人民政府外事办公室认真研析了这片古老土地上的历史文化资源和时代风貌，组织各领域权威专家学者，编译了"中华源·河南故事"中外文系列丛书，选取黄河文化、河洛文化、老子、庄子、黄帝、少林功夫、太极拳、中医、汉字、丝绸之路、古都、农业、大运河、文物、陶瓷、青铜器、手工艺、书法、杂技、豫菜、豫剧、脱贫攻坚、空中丝绸之路、航空城、南水北调、中原粮谷、红旗渠、焦裕禄等多个主题，力图以故事的方式向世界展现一个立体、全面、真实的河南。

当今世界，人类文明无论是在物质还是在精神方面都取得了巨大进步，特别是物质的极大丰富，这在古代世界是完全不能想象的。同时，当代人类也面临着许多突出的难题，比如，贫富差距持续扩大，物欲追求奢华无度，个人主义恶性膨胀，社会诚信不断消减，伦理道德每况愈下，人与自然关系日趋紧张，等等。要解决这些难题，不仅需要运用人类今天的智慧和力量，而且需要运用人类历史上积累和储存的智慧和力量。河南历史文化底蕴深厚、包容性强，在今天仍极具现实意义。中原文化蕴含的思想智慧有助于修身养性，推动人类社会进步发展，焦裕禄精神、红旗渠精神所体现的为民爱民、艰苦奋斗的价值取向是构建人类命运共同体的力量源泉。我们期待与读者们一起从河南故事中汲取更多的智慧和力量，共同创造更加美好的未来。

Series Foreword

China is one of the four ancient civilizations in the world, and is also the only country in the world where the ancient civilization has not been interrupted. Located in east-central China, Henan Province is an important cradle for the Chinese nation and Chinese civilization. In the course of the five thousand years of Chinese history, for more than three thousand years it served as the political, economic and cultural center of the country and therefore, as generally accepted, represents half of the history of China. Henan is the native place of Yellow Emperor, the cradle of Chinese culture, the starting point of the ancient Silk Road in the east, and the birthplace of Shaolin Kungfu and Chen-style Taijiquan—typical examples of the world-renowned Chinese martial arts. It was here that the earliest capital city in China was founded, the oldest Chinese characters engraved, and the earliest commerce took shape.

In the new era, Henan has witnessed rapid growth in its economy and remarkable improvement of people's living conditions owing to the national reform and opening-up policy and unremitting endeavors of the people. Modern economic achievements and social development as well as the changes of way of life could be traced back to its traditional values and cultural heritages. To enable people from other countries to understand Henan, and let the Province integrate more efficiently into the world development, the Foreign Affairs Office of the People's Government of Henan Province has organized teams of authoritative experts and scholars in relevant fields to compile this *Chinese Civilization: Stories from Henan* in Chinese and foreign languages since 2018 by crystallizing the excellence of traditions and outstanding features of modern development. The book series include *The Yellow River Culture*, *Heluo Culture*, *Laozi*, *Zhuangzi*, *The Yellow Emperor*, *Shaolin Kungfu*, *Taijiquan*, *Traditional Chinese Medicine*,

Chinese Characters, *The Silk Road*, *Ancient Chinese Capitals*, *Feeding the People—Agriculture*, *The Grand Canal*, *Cultural Heritage*, *Ceramic*, *Bronze*, *Handicraft Art*, *Calligraphy*, *Acrobatics*, *Henan Cuisine*, *Henan Opera*, *Poverty Alleviation*, *Silk Road in the Air*, *Zhengzhou—An Aviation City*, *South-to-North Water Diversion*, *Grain of the Central Plains*, *Man-Made River—Hongqiqu Canal*, *A Model Official—Jiao Yulu*, etc., presenting a panoramic picture of the Province.

In today's world, human civilization has made great progress in both material accumulation and ethical advancement, and the great abundance of materials today, especially, is beyond the imagination of the ancient people. At the same time, however, modern people are also confronted with a lot of problems, such as the widening gap between the rich and the poor, the indulgence in pursuit of luxury and extravagance, the undesirable extension of individualism, the decline of social integrity, and the increasingly tense relationship between man and nature. To solve the problems, we need to draw on the wisdom and powers developed today as well as those accumulated in the past. Henan is endowed with rich historical and cultural heritages characterized by its inclusiveness, and such heritages remain significant today. The intelligence and wisdom in Henan culture are conducive to self-cultivation and to the promotion of social development. The spirit of serving the people and relentless struggle, as embodied in Jiao Yulu and the man-made river—Hongqiqu Canal provides source of strength for building a community with a shared future for mankind. It is our hope that wisdom and strength from Henan stories could lead us to a shared brilliant future.

前　言

　　人类的发展历史，是一个不断认识自然，并通过有意识地改造自然来实现自己愿望的过程。那么，人类对天然金属的认知和利用大致是一个什么样的过程呢？以青铜器为例，人类是在利用铜这一天然金属的基础上，逐渐发展到以矿石为原料冶铸铜器的。早在史前时代，人类就采掘露天铜矿，并用获取的铜制造武器、工具和其他器皿。直到今天，铜作为与人类关系非常密切的有色金属，被广泛地应用于电气、轻工、机械制造、建筑工业、国防工业等领域。

　　冶铜术是人类的一项伟大发明创造，是世界科技史上一个重要的里程碑。在自然界中，存在着天然的纯铜，其布氏硬度仅35，可以直接锤打成器。目前我们所知的人类最早使用的红铜器，是考古学家在土耳其恰约尼遗址中发现的用自然铜矿石直接打制的钻孔珠、锥子和别针等，推测距今约1万年。在伊朗西部的艾利库什发现的用自然铜铜片卷成的小铜珠，年代也早到公元前7000年。自然铜毕竟是较少的，多数的铜要由冶炼铜矿石获得。自然界中常见的铜矿石是孔雀石。孔雀石常与自然铜一起出现，人类偶然将孔雀石投入炉火中，孔雀石中的碳酸盐受热分解，变成氧化物。氧化铜矿与木炭一起加热就能还原出铜来。有的专家推测，当这种情况重复出现多次后，人类就学会了用孔雀石和木炭冶炼红铜。人类最早使用的重要合金有砷铜和黄铜。古代西亚地区有一个较为广泛地使用砷铜的阶段，如在伊朗叶海亚发现的炼铜制品，包括刮刀、凿子等，含砷量在1.7%～3.7%，年代在公元前3800年左右。在巴勒斯坦也发现有含较多砷的铜制品，如杖首、斧、凿及饰物等，含砷量在 3.4%~12%，年代在公元前 3300 年左右。考古证明，迄今为止世界范围内共发现了公元前 5000 年至公元前 2000 年人工冶炼黄铜制品 40 余件，分布在西亚、中亚和东亚等地。中国使用铜的最早实物证明是 1973 年陕西临潼姜寨遗址出土的一件公元前 4700 年左右的半圆形残铜片，经鉴定为黄铜。史前砷铜、黄铜应由共生矿或混合矿冶炼获得，且最初采用的是固体还原工艺，经简单加工成型。共生矿或混合矿冶炼是人类早期利用金属时获得合金的一种主要方式。

我们通常所说的青铜，是指红铜加锡或其他金属的合金，其铜锈呈青绿色，因而得名。人类是在长期的实践中认识青铜的。自然铜硬度低，做成的器物易弯曲变形，人类在认识铜、利用铜的过程中逐渐了解到，如果在自然铜内加入一定比例的锡或铅等来铸造器物就能增强其硬度。铜锡或铜铅青铜有很多优点，概括起来主要有四点。一是熔点低。红铜的熔点是 1083℃，如果在其中加入一定量的锡，其熔点就会降低到 800℃~960℃，这样在熔化铜液这个环节，就会大大节约成本。二是硬度大。虽然红铜的延展性强，但布氏硬度只有 35，制成的物件太软，容易弯曲变形。若在铜液中加入锡 5%~7%，布氏硬度增至 50~60；加入锡 9%~10%，布氏硬度会达到 100。然而，锡的含量需适当，如果超过 30%，虽硬度会更大，但铸出的器件质地很脆（青铜器中锡的最大含量为 20% 左右）。三是色泽变化多。依含锡量由少到多，器物所呈现的颜色有红—橙—黄—淡黄的变化。含锡量超过 30% 时，会呈灰白色。四是流动性强。在铜液中加入一定量的铅，其流动性会更好。铜液在外范与内范（芯）之间的空腔中流动得越快，空腔中的空气就能越快排出，减少气孔，铸件不易出沙眼，便于铸造出精美的纹饰。

青铜器是指以青铜为基本原料加工制成的各类器物的总称。从目前的考古材料可知，人类很早就比较科学地掌握了铸造青铜器的合金比例。已知最早的含锡青铜器，产生于今两河流域，约在公元前 4000 年。目前在中国发现的最早的青铜器是 1975 年甘肃东乡县林家村马家窑文化遗址出土的一件青铜刀，含锡6%～10%，这件刀是用两块范闭合浇铸而成，年代约在公元前3000年。这表明，当时的居民已经掌握了锻造和铸造两种工艺技术，他们冶炼合金铜的能力，足以与同时期世界其他文明古国相媲美。

中国青铜工艺自夏代开始，经商、西周、春秋、战国乃至秦汉，具有近2000年的历史，分布范围主要集中在黄河流域和长江中下游地区，此外，还涵盖了许多边远少数民族的活动区域。

河南是中国青铜器的起源地之一，也是中国古代青铜礼乐文化的发祥地，为中国青铜文化的发展和传播做出重大贡献。河南青铜器起源早、分布广、数量多、工艺高，是中国古代青铜文化体系的重要组成部分，也是中国青铜文化萌芽、繁荣、转型进而衰落全过程的缩影，见证了中国历史从邦国发展到王国最终进入帝国的社会演进轨迹，见证了中国文明从多元到一体且以河南为中心的历史格局形成的过程，见证了中国古代族群之间以河南为中心交往、会盟、征战、婚媾、商贸等重要的历史活动。因此，河南青铜器的起源、发展的脉络在很大程度上体现了中国青铜器的发展历程。

Preface

The history of human development has been a process of knowing and modifying nature in the pursuit of human aspirations. Metallurgy has been at the core of this process. The smelting and casting of bronze wares from ore began with the exploitation of copper. As early as prehistoric times, human beings began to practice open-pit mining. The copper extracted from this industry was used to manufacture weapons, tools, and a variety of practical utensils. To this day copper is a vital non-ferrous metal that is widely used in the fields of electronics, light industry, machinery manufacturing, construction, and national defense.

Copper smelting is a great human invention and an important milestone in the world's history of technology. In nature there exists pure copper with a Brinell hardness of just 35, which can simply be hammered into tools. The earliest known red copper objects used by humans are drill beads, awls, and pins made from the natural copper ore found by archaeologists at the site of Çayoni in Turkey, around 10,000 years ago. The small beads made from rolled sheets of natural copper found at Arikush in western Iran can date back as early as 7000 BC. Copper is relatively scarce and is mostly obtained by smelting copper ore. A common copper ore found in nature is malachite. Malachite is often found together with natural copper. When by chance humans threw malachite into a furnace fire its carbonates were heated and they decomposed into oxides. Copper could be extracted when the oxidized ore was heated with charcoal. Some experts speculate that when this kind of situation was repeated many times, human beings got to learn how to smelt red copper from malachite and charcoal. Arsenical copper and brass were some of the earliest alloys. Prehistoric arsenical copper and brass were obtained by smelting the syngenetic or mixed ores, and were originally formed by a solid reduction process and simple processing. Syngenetic or mixed ore smelting was one of the main ways in which early humans obtained alloys from the use of metals. Their use was widespread throughout the ancient Near East. Copper scrapers and chisels have been found in Yahya, Iran, containing 1.7 to 3.7 percent of arsenic and dating back to around 3800 BC. Copper products containing higher levels of arsenic, such as staff heads, axes, chisels, and ornaments have also been discovered in Palestine and date back to around 3300 BC. The arsenic content of these objects ranges from 3.4 to 12 percent. Archaeological evidence suggests that more than 40 artificially smelted brass objects dating back from 5000 BC to 2000 BC have been found worldwide thus far. Many of these findings are distributed in West Asia, Central Asia, and East Asia. The earliest physical evidence of the use of brass in China comes from a semi-circular fragment dating around 4700 BC and was unearthed at the Jiangzhai site in Lintong, Shaanxi, in 1973. Prehistoric arsenopyrite and brass were obtained by smelting from syngenetic or mixed ores, and were initially formed by a solid reduction technic with simple processing. Syngenetic or mixed ore smelting was the main method with which human beings obtained alloys by using metals at the early times.

The bronze we generally refer to is an alloy of red copper with tin or other metals, which has a lime green patina, hence the name. In the process of knowing and using copper, humans gradually learned that if a certain proportion of tin or lead is added during casting, hardness can be enhanced. From this realization came the Bronze Age. Bronze is an alloy of red copper with tin or other metals and has a lime green patina. The advantages of copper-tin or copper-lead bronze can be summarized in four main points. First, its melting point is low. The melting point of red copper is 1083°C and if a certain amount of tin is added its melting point will be lowered to 800°C–960°C, so that the cost will be greatly reduced in the process of melting copper liquid. Second, it is hard. The ductility of red copper is strong but the Brinell hardness is only 35 and the objects produced are too soft, easily bent, or otherwise deformed. If 5%–7% of tin is added to the copper liquid the Brinell hardness increases to 50–60. If 9%–10% of tin is added, the Brinell hardness will reach 100. However, the content of tin has to be appropriate; if it exceeds 30%, the hardness will be even greater, but the texture of the casting device will be brittle (the maximum tin content in bronze wares is around 20%). Third, there are many variations in its color. As the tin content increases, the color of the bronze objects varies from red to orange, yellow and pale yellow respectively.

If the tin content exceeds 30%, the objects will be greyish white. Fourth, its liquidity is strong. When a certain amount of lead is added to the copper liquid, its liquidity will be better. The faster the copper liquid flows through the cavity between the outer and inner van (core), the faster the air in the cavity can be discharged, reducing porosity and making the casting less susceptible to trachoma, facilitating the casting of fine ornaments.

"Bronze ware" is the general term for all types of objects made from bronze as the basic raw material. From the available archaeological materials, it is known that mankind had an early and scientific grasp of the proportions of the alloy used to cast bronze wares. The earliest known tin-bearing bronze objects, produced in the present-day Two Rivers Valley, date back to around 4000 BC. The earliest bronze object found in China is a bronze knife cast with two van closures circa 3000 BC. It contains 6%–10% tin and was unearthed in 1975 at the Majiayao cultural site in Linjiacun, Dongxiang County, Gansu Province. This suggests that the ancient inhabitants of the area had mastered forging and casting techniques and that their ability to smelt alloy bronze was sufficient to rival that of other civilizations during the same period.

Chinese bronze craftsmanship has a history of nearly 2,000 years, starting from the Xia Dynasty, through the Shang, the Western Zhou, the Spring and Autumn, the Warring States and even the Qin and Han dynasties, with a distribution range mainly concentrated in the Yellow River basin and the middle and lower reaches of the Yangtze River and even many remote areas.

Henan made a significant contribution to the development of early Chinese bronze culture and this was expressed in bronze wares, ritual, and music. With their early origins, wide distribution, large quantity, and high craftsmanship, Henan bronze treasures remain an important part of China's rich cultural heritage. Moreover, as the following pages will demonstrate, Henan's experience in the Bronze Age bears witness to the political evolution of the Chinese state from local kingdoms to rival kingdoms and finally to empire. From this process we can see the formation of a historical pattern in Chinese civilization from pluralism to unity and Henan was in the thick of it all.

目 录   Contents

第一章　文明之光——河南青铜文化的起源和初步发展　001
　　一、青铜器在河南的出现　002
　　二、夏王朝向青铜时代的迈进　004

Chapter 1　The Light of Civilization: The Origin and Development of Bronze Culture in Henan　001
　　I. The Emergence of Bronze Wares in Henan　003
　　II. The March of the Xia Dynasty Towards the Bronze Age　005

第二章　时代绝唱——商周王朝时期河南青铜文明的鼎盛辉煌　015
　　一、王朝重器：商代青铜文化　016
　　二、制礼作乐：西周青铜文化　040
　　三、中原逐鹿：东周青铜文化　072
　　四、河南商周青铜器在世界文明史上的地位　110

Chapter 2　Greatest Hits of the Age: Henan's Bronze Civilization During the Shang and Zhou Dynasties　015
　　I. Treasures of the State: The Shang Dynasty　017
　　II. Rites and Music: The Western Zhou　041
　　III. Fighting for Supremacy in the Central Plains: The Eastern Zhou　073
　　IV. The Position of Henan's Shang and Zhou Bronze Ware in the History of World Civilization　111

第三章　百花齐放——秦汉帝国时代河南青铜艺术的转型之路　117
　　一、秦统汉继：传统礼器的延续　118
　　二、开拓创新：实用青铜器的繁荣　128

三、大道至简：实用与精神的并存转型　　142

　　四、历史选择：青铜器的没落　　154

Chapter 3　　The Blossoming of Henan's Bronze Art Under the Qin and Han Empires　　117

　　I. Inheritance and Continuity: Qin Unification and Traditional Ritual Vessels　　119

　　II. Pioneering Innovation: The Prosperity of Practical Bronze Treasures　　129

　　III. The Way to Simplicity: Practical and Spiritual Coexistence　　143

　　IV. Historical Choices: The Decline of China's Bronze Culture　　155

第四章　承传不衰——宋以来对青铜文明的追求与重建　　161

　　一、青铜礼制在宋、明、清三代的复兴　　162

　　二、以鼎为核心的青铜文化特质　　166

Chapter 4　　Rebirth: Bronze's Comeback Under the Song, Ming, and Qing Dynasties　　161

　　I. Revival of Bronze Rituals in the Song, Ming, and Qing Dynasties　　163

　　II. Unique Traits of Ding as the Core of the Bronze Culture　　167

结　语　　174

Conclusion　　175

附录：中国历史年代简表　　176

Appendix: A Brief Chronology of Chinese History　　176

第一章

文明之光——河南青铜文化的起源和初步发展

Chapter 1

The Light of Civilization: The Origin and Development of Bronze Culture in Henan

一、青铜器在河南的出现

考古发现表明，在河南境内的一些龙山文化（公元前2500—前2000年）遗址中出土有青铜冶炼的遗物。例如，郑州董砦遗址曾出土有青铜片，郑州牛砦遗址和汝州煤山遗址均发现有炼铜用的坩埚，登封王城岗遗址出土了一件青铜容器的残片，淮阳平粮台古城遗址内发现了一块铜炼渣等。河南出土的龙山文化时代的青铜器品种较少，多属于日常工具和生活类器物，如刀、锥、钻、环等。这些青铜制品通常采用合范的方法铸造而成，其工艺虽较为简单，但从中可以看出，先民们对自然界的铜、铅、锡等金属矿物及其合金比例的认知，经历了长期的实践和探索。可以说，青铜器的出现及其所反映的生产力水平，是人类进入文明社会的一个重要特征。

I. The Emergence of Bronze Wares in Henan

Relics of bronze smelting in Henan have been unearthed at sites belonging to the ancient Longshan Culture (2500-2000 BC). In Zhengzhou, the archeological evidence includes bronze flakes excavated from the Dongzhai site and crucibles for copper smelting at the Niuzhai site. Crucibles have also been found at the Meishan site in Ruzhou. A fragment of a bronze object was excavated from the Wangchenggang site in Dengfeng, and a piece of copper smelting slag has been found at the ancient city of Pingliangtai in Huaiyang. The bronze objects from the Longshan Culture excavated in Henan mostly consist of everyday tools and household objects such as knives, awls, drills and rings. These objects were cast using the mould-combining method. Although the process was relatively simple, these artifacts demonstrate that the Longshan Culture enjoyed a long period of practice in the ideal proportions of copper, lead, tin and other metal minerals and their alloys. The products of these skilled craftsmen marked mankind's entry into civilization.

二、夏王朝向青铜时代的迈进

众所周知,我们的祖先以卓越的智慧和辛勤的劳动,创造了举世瞩目的华夏文明。河南省简称豫,得名于古代九州中的豫州。因处天下之中,史称中原。中原大地有着前后相承的文化血脉,史前文化在此不断碰撞与融合,最先诞生了国家——夏。夏代是中国历史上第一个世袭王朝。史学家们大多将夏代的开始从夏禹算起。自禹至桀,共十四代、十七王,前后经过了400余年(约公元前2070—前1600年)。但是由于史料的缺乏,长期以来,夏代的许多史实还不够清楚,夏代的文化面貌还存在不少疑问。从20世纪50年代开始,河南偃师二里头遗址的持续发掘,以及中原诸多夏代遗存的发现,揭开了中国第一个王朝夏代的神秘面纱,证明了约公元前21世纪夏王朝在中原建都的史实。河南偃师二里头遗址的考古发现表明,这里是夏代晚期的都城遗址(公元前1750—前1550年)。

偃师二里头遗迹分布图
Erlitou Site, Yanshi

II. The March of the Xia Dynasty Towards the Bronze Age

Chinese civilization emerged among several tribes, the most significant of which settled around the middle and lower reaches of the Yellow River. Henan Province, known as Yu for short, was named after the state of Yu among nine ancient states. Throughout history it has also been known as the Central Plains because of its geographical location in the center of China. Within the Central Plains, prehistoric cultures collided and fused, giving birth to the first Chinese nation, the Xia. The Xia Dynasty (1750-1550 BC) was the first hereditary dynasty in Chinese history. Most historians reckon the beginning of the Xia Dynasty from its founder Xia Yu. From Yu to Jie, there were fourteen generations and seventeen kings, spanning more than 400 years (around 2070-1600 BC). However, due to a lack of historical records, much about the Xia Dynasty remains unknown. Nonetheless, excavations that have taken place since the 1950's at the Erlitou site in Yanshi, Henan Province, coupled with the discovery of many Xia Dynasty remains in the Central Plains have proven the historicity of the Xia Dynasty. These excavations have even established its capital in the Central Plains to have existed from around the 21st century BC.

The writings of ancient historians and discoveries at Erlitou show that bronze culture was a feature of the Xia. *Zuo Zhuan – The Third Year of the Duke of Xuan* states, "In the old days when the Xia Dynasty had just installed a virtuous ruler, images of strange things from afar were depicted, and nine cauldrons were cast from the metal tribute from the nine states, reflecting all the things depicted on the cauldrons." In *The Records of the Grand Historian – The Record of Emperor Xiaowu*, it is stated that "During the Xia Dynasty, chiefs from other states paid tribute to Dayu in metal, which he used to forge nine large cauldrons." These documents tell that Dayu conquered all the floods of the land. In recognition of this feat, all the tribes elected him as their leader. Then, he divided the world into nine states and made the governors of the states pay him tribute in bronze which he had forged into nine cauldrons. The nine cauldrons were engraved with images of famous mountains, rivers, and exotic objects from the nine states. One cauldron was used to symbolize one state, and the nine cauldrons were centralized in the

青铜器作为中国古代文明的标志性成就，应该是从夏代开始的。《左传·宣公三年》曰"昔夏之方有德也，远方图物，贡金九牧，铸鼎象物，百物而为之备"。《史记·孝武本纪》有载"禹收九牧之金，铸九鼎"。这些文献表明，大禹治理水患成功后，华夏诸族推他为领袖。大禹划分天下为九州，令九州州长贡献青铜，铸造九鼎，将全国九州的名山大川、奇异之物的图像刻于九鼎之身。以一鼎象征一州，并将九鼎集中于夏王朝都城。禹铸九鼎一方面反映了全国的统一和王权的高度集中，显示夏王已成为天下共主，另一方面说明大禹时期开启了中国青铜时代的大门。

传说中大禹铸的九鼎如今已无迹可寻，但考古工作者在中原大地上的二里头遗址这一夏代都城内发现了制作青铜器的作坊，作坊中出土有炼渣、炼铜坩埚和陶范残片。此外，在遗址中还发现了一些青铜酒器、兵器和乐器。这些青铜器包括凿、锥、刀、镞、戈、戚等工具和兵器，嵌松石兽面纹铜牌饰、纺轮、鱼钩、泡等装饰品，还有鼎、盉、斝、爵等容器，以及铃等乐器。

虽然鼎、盉、爵等青铜容器仅发现数十件，但在青铜铸造史上极为重要。这些青铜容器是采用范铸法制作而成的。范铸法是以范组合成铸型，再浇铸铜液成器，其制作过程是：1.用经过淘洗的陶土塑制成一件与欲铸的容器一样的模型，并在上面刻上花纹，然后阴凉烘干，成为陶模。2.用陶土加细沙等和成泥片包压在陶模之上，然后用刀子划开制成几块外范，各块外范之间有榫卯相套合。3.用泥依陶模形状，减去容器的壁厚，制成内范（芯）。4.将入窑烘热、成为陶质的内范（芯）与外范组装在一起，外面用泥及绳索包裹固定后，浇铸青铜液。待铜液凝固后，打碎外范，取出内范（芯），取出青铜器，并加以打磨修整，一件青铜容器就铸成了。

由此可见，以二里头遗址为代表的夏代青铜工艺，从制作简单的工具、兵器到铸造复杂的容器，制作方式已经由锻造或单范铸造进入技术含量高的复合范铸造阶段，这在生产技术上是一次飞跃。这些青铜器具

capital of the Xia Dynasty. Dayu's casting of the nine cauldrons symbolizes the unification of the country and the centralization of royal power by representing that the leader of the Xia had become the master of his world. It also credits Dayu with opening the door to the Bronze Age in China.

The legendary nine cauldrons forged by Dayu are nowhere to be found today but archaeologists have discovered a bronze workshop at the Erlitou where slag, copper crucibles, and pottery fragments have been unearthed. In addition, a number of bronze drinking vessels, weapons, and musical instruments have been found at the site. These include tools and weapons such as chisels, awls, knives, arrowheads, goshawks, tomahawks, decorative items such as bronze medallion with inlaid turquoise of animal textures, spinning wheels, fishing hooks and bubbles, as well as vessels such as cauldrons, divorces, jars and jugs, and musical instruments such as bells.

The vessels were made using the mould-casting method. The process was as follows: 1. The panned clay was used to make a mould, a pattern was carved into it, and then cooled and dried. 2. Fine sand was added to make a clay sheet to be pressed on top of the clay mould to be cut with a knife to make several pieces of the outer mould. A combination of tenon and mortise was added to the outer mould. 3. The clay was used in accordance with the shape of the pottery mould (minus the wall thickness of the container) to make the inner mould (core). 4. After being put into a kiln for baking, the ceramic inner mould (core) was assembled with the outer mould, which was wrapped, fixed with clay and rope, and cast with bronze liquid. When the bronze liquid had solidified, the outer mould was broken, and the inner mould (core) removed. The bronze was then taken out, polished, and trimmed.

It can be seen that the bronze craftsmanship of the Xia Dynasty had developed from the production of simple tools and weapons to the casting of complex vessels. The production method had moved from forging or single mould-casting to the highly technical stage of composite mould-casting. This was a leap forward in production technology. These bronze wares had such functions as containers, weapons and musical instruments, reflecting the development of a ritual system and social hierarchy. The discovery of a large-scale bronze casting workshop at Erlitou with the excavation of bronze wares indisputably established

备了容器、兵器、乐器等功能，反映了礼制、社会等级制度的进一步发展。二里头遗址内规模宏大的铸铜作坊遗址的发现和成组青铜容器的出土，无可置疑地证明二里头文化已经进入青铜时代。

夏史物证——铜器一组

方格纹铜鼎
Bronze Ding Tripod with Check Designs

方格纹铜鼎，夏代，洛阳博物馆藏。这是二里头遗址目前出土的唯一一件青铜鼎，也是所见时代最早的一件铜鼎。鼎是中国青铜文化的代表，被称为"国之重器"，是国家和权力的象征。它的得与失，往往是一个国家兴衰的标志。这件具备礼器功能的青铜鼎，是二里头遗址为中国最早的王权国家都邑的实物例证。

铜爵
Bronze Jue

Erlitou culture in the Bronze Age.

Bronze Ding Tripod with Check Design, Xia Dynasty, in the collection of the Luoyang Museum. This is the only bronze cauldron ever unearthed at the Erlitou site, and it is the earliest one of its age ever seen. The cauldron is a representative of Chinese bronze culture and is known as a "national treasure", a symbol of state and power. Its success or failure is often a sign of the rise or fall of a nation. This bronze cauldron, with its ritualistic function, is a physical example of the Erlitou site being the earliest capital of royalty in China.

Bronze Jue, Xia Dynasty, excavated from the Erlitou site, in the collection of the Institute of Archaeology, Chinese Academy of Social Sciences. Its basic features are a long and narrow stream, a long and pointed tail, a short double column, a girdled waist, a flat base, a three-legged undercarriage, and a raised belly. This is the earliest bronze drinking vessel in China. Its streamlined body, with its long flowing mouth and blade-like pointed tail forming a balanced confrontation, is slender and simple overall, reflecting the deep and unique sense of beauty of the ancestors.

Bronze Bells, Xia Dynasty, excavated from the Erlitou site, in the collection of the Institute of Archaeology, Chinese Academy of Social Sciences. Four bronze bells were unearthed during the archaeological excavations at the Erlitou site from 1981 to 1986. These bells are of similar forms, narrow at the top and wide at the bottom, with a hinged tile shape in their cross-sections, with one side of the bell body with a casual rib and two holes at the top, and a bridge-shaped button in the middle. The entire body is plain, with traces of weaving on the surface. The oval body of the bell is inherited from the oval body of the pottery bell, an ancient musical instrument from the Central Plains, and, as a precursor to the oval Chinese bronze bells, it has laid the foundation for the shape of the bronze instrument in the Shang Dynasty. When this bell was unearthed, there was a tubular jade tongue inside the bell cavity, and the bell and tongue were matched just perfectly, obviously making it an extremely valuable object at the time.

铜爵，夏代，二里头遗址出土，中国社会科学院考古研究所藏。其基本的特点是窄长流、尖长尾、矮小双柱、束腰、平底，底下承三足，腹部有一錾。这是中国最早的青铜饮酒器。它流线型的器身上，长流口与叶片状的尖尾形成均衡的对峙，整体纤秀而简洁，反映出先民对美的深切而独特的感觉。

铜铃
Bronze Bell

铜铃，夏代，二里头遗址出土，中国社会科学院考古研究所藏。1981—1986年在二里头遗址的考古发掘中，先后有4只铜铃出土。这些铃的形制相近，上部窄下部宽，横断面为合瓦形，铃体一侧有扉棱，顶有两孔，中间有桥形钮。通体素面，器表附有纺织痕迹。铜铃的合瓦形铃体继承了中原地区古乐器陶铃的椭圆体，作为中国合瓦形铜钟形制的先源，它奠定了商周青铜乐器造型的基础。这件铜铃出土时，铃腔内有一管状玉质铃舌，铃、舌金玉相配，可见在当时为极其珍贵的物品。

镶嵌绿松石兽面纹铜牌饰，夏代，二里头遗址出土，二里头夏都遗址博物馆藏。铜牌饰呈长圆形，中间呈弧状，束腰，近似鞋底形，两侧各有二穿孔钮，凸面有许多不同形状的绿松石片粘嵌排成兽面纹，凹面附着有麻布纹。图案美观，立体感强，制作精巧且保存完好，集铸造与

镶嵌绿松石兽面纹铜牌饰
Bronze Plate Inlaid with Turquoise Animal Face Design

Bronze Plate Inlaid with Turquoise Animal Face Design, Xia Dynasty, excavated from the Erlitou site, in the collection of the Erlitou Site Museum of the Xia Capital. The bronze medallion is oblong in shape, curved in the middle and girdled, resembling the shape of a shoe sole, with two perforated buttons on each side, the convex side with a number of turquoise pieces of different shapes glued together in a bestial pattern, the concave side with a linen pattern. The design is beautiful, three-dimensional, exquisitely crafted and well preserved, combining casting and inlay techniques, making it a rare bronze art object. The ornate bronze plaque decoration, together with the lacquered drum and bronze bell, suggests that it was not an ordinary ornament, but rather a vessel used by shamans or aristocrats with ritual powers to perform primitive religious activities such as sacrificing to the gods and exorcising evil spirits.

镶嵌工艺于一身，是难得的青铜艺术珍品。华美的铜牌饰与漆鼓、铜铃在一起，表明它绝非一般饰物，当与祭祀、通神有关，应是巫师或有祭祀权的贵族进行祭祀通神、厌胜驱邪等原始宗教活动的法器。

根据目前的考古发现，夏代青铜器一开始就具备了容器、兵器、乐器等功能，见证了中国青铜时代"器以藏礼"的特性。夏代的青铜器体积一般都比较小，器壁很薄；种类较少，器型也比较简单；大多素面，或者只是装饰个别圆点或者圆饼或者几道单线。由此看来，夏代是中国进入青铜时代的初期，青铜铸造业还不够发达。

According to current archaeological findings, the bronze objects of the Xia Dynasty functioned as containers, weapons and musical instruments from the very beginning, testifying the characteristics of "vessels hiding rites" during the Chinese Bronze Age. The bronze objects of the Xia Dynasty are generally small in size, with thin walls, fewer types and simpler shapes. And they are mostly plain in appearance, either decorated with individual dots or round cakes or just a few single lines. Therefore, it can be seen that the Xia Dynasty was the initial stage of the Bronze Age in China and that the bronze casting industry was not yet well developed.

第二章

时代绝唱——商周王朝时期河南青铜文明的鼎盛辉煌

Chapter 2

Greatest Hits of the Age: Henan's Bronze Civilization During the Shang and Zhou Dynasties

河南向来被视为中国文明起源的中心地区，也是中国青铜器最发达的地区。尤其是在中国青铜文化最为辉煌的商周时期，河南是商王朝和东周王室的定都之地，也是商周时期诸侯王国分布最为密集的地区，郑州商代都城、安阳殷墟和洛阳东周王城等都是当时重要的青铜铸造中心。河南出土的大量青铜器，种类丰富、造型独特、工艺精湛，代表了当时中国青铜冶铸的最高水平。由于当时青铜材质的稀有和青铜器铸造工艺的复杂，商周时期的青铜器成为王室和诸侯贵族的专属用品和礼仪等级的象征，对当时中国的社会政治产生了巨大影响。

一、王朝重器：商代青铜文化

公元前 16 世纪，商汤起兵灭夏，建立商朝。从商汤立国至公元前 1046 年纣王灭国，共历十七代、三十一王。河南是商王朝统治的核心区域，商朝存在的 500 多年间曾五次迁都，五个都城中的四个都在河南境内。目前在河南偃师、郑州、安阳都发现了商代具有王都规模的遗址。此外，在河南的大部分地区都发现有商代文化遗存。商人敬神崇鬼，开始使用成体系的文字，铸造大量的青铜器，将中国的青铜文明推向了高峰。

与夏代相比，商代铸铜业有了显著的进步，除工具和兵器外，容器有十多种，主要是盛食器、酒器、水器等。河南商代青铜器主要出土于郑州商城、安阳殷墟这两个具有王都规模的遗址，在登封、中牟、新郑、辉县、温县、正阳、罗山等地也有零星发现。

1. 郑州商城的商代前期青铜器

郑州商城遗址发现于 1950 年，是商代前期的都城遗址，总面积约 25 平方公里，是一处规划缜密、布局完整的大型都邑，始建于公元前 1600 年左右。城址的平面近似长方形，有内城、外城两重城垣。内城城墙周长约 7 公里。城址包括宫殿区、手工业作坊区、居民区、墓葬区

Henan was at the heart and center of early Chinese civilization and was the most developed region in bronze treasures. In particular, during the Shang and Zhou dynasties, the most glorious periods of Chinese bronze culture, Henan was the capital of the Shang Dynasty and the Eastern Zhou royal family, and was also the most densely distributed area of the Shang and Zhou vassal states. In those days, the Zhengzhou Shang capital, Anyang Yin Ruins and the Eastern Zhou royal city in Luoyang, were all important bronze casting centers. A large number of bronze wares excavated in Henan, with their rich variety, unique shapes and exquisite craftsmanship, represent the highest level of bronze smelting and casting in China at that time. Due to the scarcity of bronze materials and the complexity of the bronze casting process, the bronze wares of the Shang and Zhou periods became the exclusive objects and symbols of ritual rank for the royal family and vassal nobility, and had a great impact on the social politics of China at the time.

I. Treasures of the State: The Shang Dynasty

In the 16th century BC, a rebellion of the Shang under their leader Tang, destroyed the Xia Dynasty and established the Shang Dynasty. From King Tang's establishment of the Shang Dynasty to King Zhou's destruction of the dynasty in 1046 BC, there were seventeen generations and thirty-one kings. Henan was the central area of the Shang Dynasty's reign and the capital was transferred five times during the 500 years of the Shang Dynasty's existence, with four of the five capitals located in Henan. The capital sites of the Shang Dynasty have been found in Yanshi, Zhengzhou, and Anyang. In addition, the cultural remains from the Shang Dynasty have been found throughout Henan. The people of the Shang Dynasty revered gods and ghosts, used systematic writing, cast a large number of bronze treasures, pushing China's bronze civilization to its peak.

Compared with the Xia, the Shang made significant progress in bronze casting. In addition to tools and weapons, they cast ten types of bronze wares, most prominently food, wine, and water vessels. Bronze wares found in Henan from the Shang Dynasty were mainly excavated in Zhengzhou and Anyang Yin Ruins. They were also found scattered in Dengfeng, Zhongmu, Xinzheng, Huixian, Wenxian, Zhengyang, Luoshan, and other places.

几部分，在城址内发现了大批具有王室性质的青铜礼器。

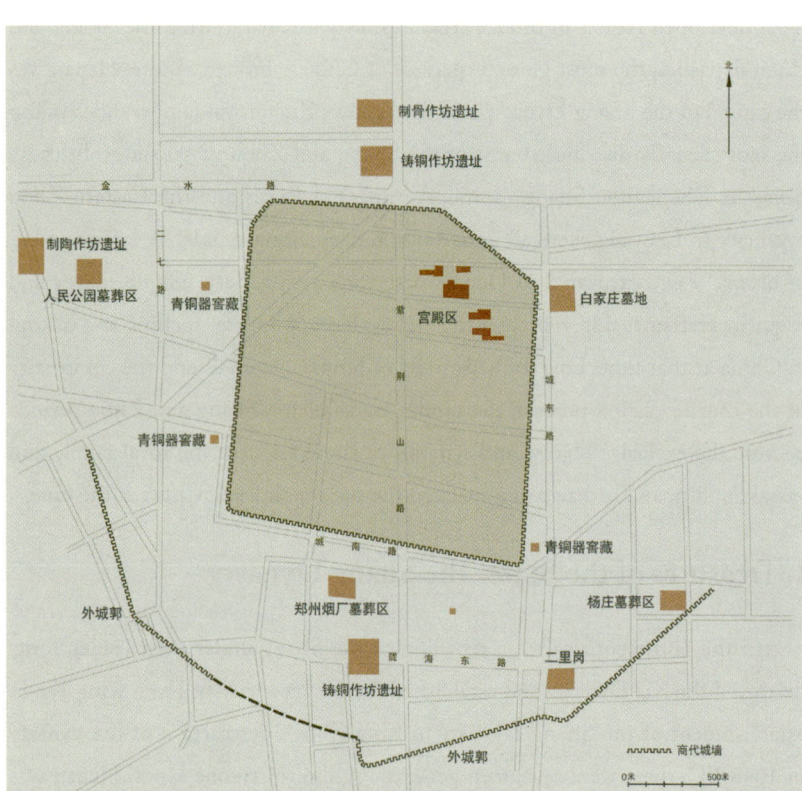

郑州商城平面图
Shangcheng Ruins of Zhengzhou, Shang Dynasty

在郑州商城南关外和紫荆山北发现了两处铸铜作坊遗址。南关外铸铜遗址发现有铸铜场地以及熔铜炉残片、炼铜坩埚和陶范残片、炼渣、炭屑、矿石等铸铜遗物。

郑州商城出土的商代前期青铜器极具代表性。在郑州二里冈、白家庄、南关外、铭功路、二七路等地的10余处商代前期贵族墓葬中，出土了一批精美的青铜器。此外，1974—1996年，在郑州商城内城墙外侧的杜岭街、向阳回族食品厂、南顺城街发现了三个商代前期的青铜窖藏坑。

1. Bronze Treasures from Zhengzhou in the Early Shang Dynasty

Discovered in 1950, the Shang site of Zhengzhou was a capital site of the early Shang Dynasty, covering a total area of about 25 square kilometers, which was also a meticulously planned and fully laid-out grand capital built around 1600 BC. The capital site is approximately rectangular, with two walls forming the inner city and the outer city. The inner city wall is approximately 7km in circumference. The site includes a palace area, a craft workshop area, a residential area and a burial area. A large number of bronze ritual objects with royal characteristics have been found within the site.

Two copper-casting workshops were discovered at the Shang site of Zhengzhou: South Outskirts and North Zijingshan. The copper casting site at the South Outskirts was found to contain copper casting areas as well as copper casting relics such as fragments of copper melting furnaces, copper smelting crucibles and pottery mould fragments, slag, carbon chips and ore.

The bronze wares of the early Shang Dynasty excavated in Zhengzhou are highly representative. A number of exquisite bronze treasures have been unearthed from more than 10 noble burials of the early Shang Dynasty in Erligang, Baijiazhuang, South Outskirts, Minggong Road, and Erqi Road in Zhengzhou. In addition, in the years 1974-1996, three bronze cellar pits of the early Shang Dynasty were discovered on Duling Street, Xiangyang Food Factory of Hui Ethnic Group and South Shuncheng Street, outside the inner city walls of the Shang site in Zhengzhou.

The pit contains 28 bronze wares, including square *ding*, round *ding*, Tiliang wine containers and bull-head shaped drinking vessels. These bronze wares were all buried outside the city on high grounds very close to the city walls and placed in certain patterns. The floors of the cellars have been decorated or furnished, some of which are covered with wooden slabs and vermilion, and some of which are found containing ash pits buried with cattle skeletons in their vicinity. The most important of these ritual vessels was the *ding*. The bronze *ding*, as an important representative of bronze ritual vessels, also underwent significant changes in form during the early Shang Dynasty. In addition to the round bronze cauldrons, some new sets of square ones also appeared, and the ornaments on

郑州商城遗址青铜窖藏坑发掘现场
Excavation Site of the Bronze Cellar at Shangcheng Ruins, Zhengzhou

坑内有方鼎、圆鼎、提梁卣、牛首尊等 28 件青铜器。这些青铜器均埋在城外距城墙很近的高地上，按一定规律放置。窖藏内的地面经过加工，有的还铺有木板和朱砂；有的窖藏附近还发现了埋有牛骨架的灰坑，因而推测这些窖藏青铜器应是商王室举行祭祀的礼器。这些礼器中最重要仍是鼎。青铜鼎作为青铜礼器的重要代表，其形制在商代前期也发生了很大变化，除圆形鼎外，新出现了成套的方形铜鼎，鼎上的纹饰由夏代的以线条组成的简单纹样，发展成较为复杂的兽面图案。三处窖藏坑中共发现 8 件大方鼎，其中杜岭街的窖藏坑中出土的 1 号鼎（乳钉纹青铜方鼎）最大，通高 100 厘米、口长 62.5 厘米、口宽 61 厘米，重 86.4 千克，风格古朴端庄，器身铸有精美的纹饰，是目前已发现的商代前期青铜器中体积最大的。这件鼎体形高大，铸造难度也大。铸型共用范、芯 20 多块，先铸腹壁和鼎耳，再铸鼎底并和腹壁相接，最后铸鼎足并与鼎底相接。在它身上，中国商代青铜铸造工艺的分铸和拼铸技术结合得尽善尽美。大家可以想象，铜在当时是非常贵重的金属，且制作

the cauldrons developed from the simple pattern of lines of the Xia Dynasty to a more complex pattern of animal faces. A total of eight large cauldrons were found in the three pits, of which Cauldron No. 1 (Bronze Rectangular Ding with Boss Designs) is the largest bronze rectangular *ding* with boss designs, 100cm high, 62.5cm long, 61cm wide, and weighing 86.4 kg, and is of a simple and dignified style, with fine ornaments cast into the body. It is the largest of the early Shang Dynasty bronze wares ever found, and its large size made it difficult to cast. In the process of bronze cauldron casting, a total of more than 20 moulds and cores were used, with the ventral walls and ears cast first, the base cast and joined to the ventral walls then, and the feet cast and joined to the base finally. Here, the split and combined casting techniques of the Shang Dynasty bronze casting craftsmanship are perfectly displayed. Copper was a very precious metal at the time and the production of such a large bronze vessel required a great deal of human, material, and financial resources. Only those who possessed great power could manipulate copper and labor resources through advanced and complex ruling networks.

The early Shang made significant improvements over the Xia in the casting of bronze weapons and tools in both quality and variety. In addition to the original types of jugs, jars, divorces, and round cauldrons, there appeared some new varieties such as rectangular *ding*, *li* (ancient cooking tripot), *gui* (ancient food vessel), *yan* (ancient cooking utensil), *gu* (wine vessel), *zun*, *lei* (wine container), *you* (wine container), plates, and pots. The predominance of bronze ritual vessels dating from the period indicates that the ancient Chinese bronze ritual vessel system was fully formed under the Shang. The Shang expanded the Xia's practice of combined-function wares breaking ground with such combinations as jugs and jars, jugs and divorces, jugs and goblets, and jug earthenware plates. The jug-jar combinations are the most predominant among the discoveries. The walls of the bronze vessels are thicker than those in the Xia Dynasty, the bellies deeper, the feet more often pointed and tapered, and the rims of goblets, *zun*, earthenware and plates shorter, with cross-shaped openings. In the early Shang Dynasty, bronze wares were often decorated with ornaments—a beast's face in bold lines was a common feature. In addition, there were also human representations: *kui*, dragons, tigers, thunderbolts, clouds, triangular thunderbolts, vortexes, nipples, etc. However, the ornaments were still relatively simple, often consisting of a single

如此大的青铜器，需要花费大量的人力、物力和财力，只有具有强大权力的人才能通过高级而复杂的统治网络来支配铜资源和劳动资源。

商代前期的青铜兵器、工具等相比夏代有明显改进，青铜容器种类增加较多，除了原有器种爵、斝、盉、圆鼎外，新出现了方鼎、鬲、簋、甗、觚、尊、罍、卣、盘、盂等。青铜礼器占主导地位，表明中国古代青铜礼器系统基本形成。青铜器的组合形式多样，较夏代丰富，级别层次也趋复杂，有爵斝、爵盉、斝爵觚、爵觚、鼎斝爵觚、鼎鬲斝爵罍盘等，但仍以爵斝组合为主。器壁较夏代为厚，器腹较深，足多作尖锥足，觚、尊、罍、盘等器的圈足较矮，上有"十"字形镂孔。商代前期青铜器普遍施有纹饰，纹饰主体是以粗犷线条构成的兽面纹。此外，还有人字纹、夔纹、龙纹、虎纹、目雷纹、云纹、三角雷纹、涡纹、乳钉纹等，装饰渐趋繁缛。但总体来说，纹饰的形式还较为简单，主要流行单层的线刻花纹。本期青铜器上的铭文极为少见，仅为单个日名或族徽。商代前期的青铜器制作较之夏代，已经可以成熟使用复合陶范技术，并出现了分铸（铸接）技术，如大方鼎、大圆鼎等大型礼器常用多范、分铸、嵌铸、分次浇铸的铸造方法。但从整体看，尚未达到成熟阶段，如鼎、斝等三足器，其一耳与一足呈垂直线，造型显得不平衡等。

商代前期是中国青铜文化走向繁荣的重要时期。这一时期的青铜器较夏代有很大进步，不仅种类和数量有所增加，冶铸技术、装饰工艺也表现出较高的水平。青铜器的造型和纹饰，给人一种狞厉、威严之感，透露出与商王朝统治权力一样的神秘气氛，彰显了商王至高无上的统治权威。这也是国家在始创时期，人们对国家机器巨大能力的神秘化反映。

2. 安阳殷墟的商代后期青铜器

公元前 1300 年，盘庚迁都于殷（今安阳市），至纣王（帝辛）亡国，整个商代后期以此为都，共经八代、十二王，250 余年。1899 年王懿荣先生首次确认安阳出土有甲骨文，1928 年在此进行首次考古发掘。

乳钉纹青铜方鼎
Bronze Rectangular Ding with Boss Designs

layer of line engraving. The inscriptions on bronze wares of this issue are rather few, consisting only of a single day, name, or family crest. Compared with the Xia, the techniques of making bronze wares in the early Shang were already mature enough to use composite pottery moulding techniques, and the technique of split-casting (casting and jointing) had emerged as well. These were steady advances but Chinese bronze casting was (as of yet) far from its most mature stage. We can see from the cauldron, jar, and some of the other three-legged vessels that simple vertical lines were used to form the ears and feet and the shapes appear to be unbalanced.

In summary, Chinese bronze culture flourished under the early Shang. The bronze wares of the period showed great progress over the innovations of the Xia, not only in terms of the increasing varieties and quantities, but also in terms of higher levels of smelting and casting techniques and decorative craftsmanship. The shapes and ornamental patterns of early Shang bronze objects display a sense of sternness and majesty, highlighting the supreme authority and mystique of the Shang kings.

2. Bronze Treasures of the Late Shang Dynasty from the Yin Ruins in Anyang

Oracle bone inscriptions were first identified by Wang Yirong in 1899 and the first archaeological excavation was carried out in Anyang in 1928. This was

经过90多年、几代考古学者的不懈努力，在安阳洹河两岸约24平方公里的范围内发现并发掘了宫殿宗庙区、王陵区、祭祀场所、墓葬区、手工业作坊和居民区，出土了数以万计的铜、陶、玉、石、骨、蚌等遗物和十万多片甲骨，埋藏了3000多年的商代晚期都城的秘密逐步被揭开。

盘庚迁殷后的250多年，商代政治中心未有大的迁移，为青铜业的发展营造了稳定的社会环境，河南青铜器进入第一个蓬勃发展时期。考古工作者在安阳殷墟发现了多处铸铜作坊遗址，并且这些遗址有规律地分布于殷墟遗址内。如，在西部的孝民屯、南部的苗圃北地、东部的大司空、中部的小屯宫殿区等地均发现有铸铜作坊遗址。这些作坊集中分布有利于技术的传承，便于王室管理和控制。

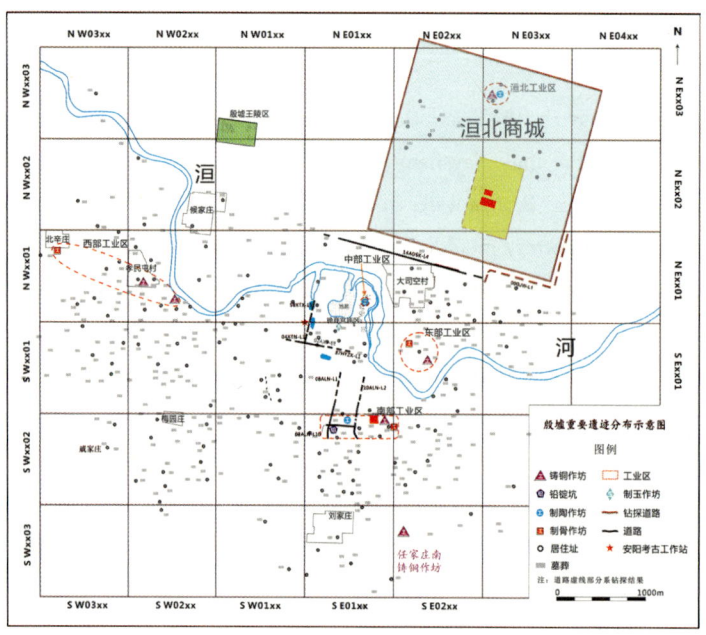

殷墟重要遗迹分布图

Major Sites of the Yin Ruins, Anyang

the site of the late Shang Dynasty's capital (Yin), transferred there by King Pan Geng in 1300 BC where it remained for more than 250 years until the end of the dynasty. After more than 90 years of unremitting efforts by several generations of archaeologists, palaces, temples, royal tombs, places of worship, craft workshops, and residential areas have been discovered and excavated in an area of about 24 square kilometers on both sides of the Huan River in Anyang, and tens of thousands of relics of copper, pottery, jade, stone, bone, mussel, and more than 100,000 pieces of oracle bones have been unearthed. Some of the secrets of the late Shang Dynasty capital, buried for over 3,000 years, have been uncovered.

In the centuries that followed Pan Geng's transferring of the capital to Yin, the political center of the Shang Dynasty did not move significantly and this created a stable social environment for the flourishing of Henan bronze treasures. Archaeologists have discovered a number of bronze workshops at the Yin Ruins in Anyang. Copper-casting workshop sites were found in Xiaomintun in the west, the northern part of the Miao Pu area in the south, Dasikong in the east, and the Xiaotun palace area in the center. The centralized distribution of these workshops facilitated the transmission of technology and made it convenient for the royal family to manage and control.

The copper casting sites are large in scale, among which the northern part of the Miao Pu copper casting site covers an area of over 10,000 square meters, with five furnaces, over 5,000 fragments, 90 crucible fragments, and over 20,000 pottery moulds and models found. The external moulds are mainly ceremonial, with fewer tool and weapon moulds. These bronze casting sites have provided important physical information for academic research into the process, production techniques, organization, and management of bronze casting at Yin Ruins.

It is worth noting that in 2015 a late Shang Dynasty storage pit containing nearly 300 lead ingots with a total weight of 3.32 tonnes was discovered in the north ground of Liujiazhuang at Yin Ruins, some 300 meters west of the copper casting workshop in the northern ground of Miao Pu.

In 2016, another bronze ritual casting workshop of unprecedented scale was discovered in the west of Xindian Village, to the northeast of Yin Ruins, 10 kilometers away from the Xiaotun palace area. The excavations revealed a total of 40 Shang Dynasty tombs, 63 ash pits, five housing sites, two kiln sites, two roads,

铸铜遗址规模较大，其中苗圃北地铸铜遗址面积有 10000 平方米以上，发现有熔炉 5 座，残块 5000 多块，坩埚残片 90 多块，陶范和陶模 20000 多块。外范以礼器范为主，工具范和兵器范较少。这些铸铜遗址为学术界研究殷墟铸铜的工艺流程、生产技术、组织管理等诸多问题提供了重要的实物资料。

值得一提的是，2015 年，在殷墟刘家庄北地发现一座商代晚期埋藏近 300 块、总重量达 3.32 吨铅锭的贮藏坑，该贮藏坑东距苗圃北地铸铜作坊约 300 米。显然，这是铸铜作坊区重要的备料贮藏坑，由此可见铸铜手工业生产规模之大。

铅锭贮藏坑
Lead Cellar

2016 年，在殷墟东北、距离小屯宫殿区 10 公里的辛店村西发现了又一处规模空前的青铜礼器铸造作坊。此次发掘共发现商代墓葬 40 座，灰坑 63 处，房址 5 处，窑址 2 处，道路 2 条，以及铸铜相关遗迹多处。遗址内出土近千件陶范、磨石、窑壁、炉壁等与铸铜相关的遗迹遗物，这个铸铜作坊与殷墟已发现的铸铜遗址相同，都是当时青铜礼器重要的生产基地。

以安阳殷墟文化为代表的商代后期，是我国青铜器铸造的第一个高峰期。这时人们掌握了更为先进的铸造工艺，制造出令人叹为观止的重器。殷墟青铜器大部分出自墓葬，居址和祭祀遗址中也有少量发现。殷

and several sites related to bronze casting. Nearly 1,000 pieces of pottery moulds, grinding stones, kiln walls, furnace walls and other relics related to bronze casting were unearthed at the site, and this bronze casting workshop was the same as the bronze casting site previously found at Yin Ruins, which were both important production bases for bronze ceremonial wares at the time.

The late Shang Dynasty, represented by the Yin Ruins culture of Anyang, was the first peak of bronze casting in China. This was a time when its people mastered more advanced casting techniques and produced breathtakingly precious wares. Most of the Yin Ruins bronze wares were unearthed from tombs, and a small number of them were found at some dwelling sites and sacrificial sites. According to their functions, the bronze wares at Yin Ruins can be divided into ritual vessels, musical instruments, weapons, production tools, household utensils, works of art, carriages and miscellaneous objects. The most famous of these is the large Houmuwu Cauldron, excavated in the royal tomb area of Yin Ruins, which is 133cm high, 112cm long, 79.2cm wide, and weighs 832.84 kg, making it the heaviest bronze ware now known from ancient China. The Houmuwu Cauldron has a thunder pattern around the body and is decorated with coiled dragons and animal-face motifs, with a majestic form, complex structure, magnificent ornaments, and excellent workmanship, displaying a high level of techniques and making it a masterpiece of bronze ware at the time.

The excavation of Fuhao's tomb in 1976 was one of the most important discoveries at Anyang Yin Ruins. It was the burial place of a woman of high stature and research has suggested that she was the wife of King Wu Ding of the Shang. Nearly 2,000 treasures of exquisite quality and high value were found there. Questions have arisen about who she was and why she was honored so extravagantly after death. The answers have been found in the oracle bones of the Yin Ruins. There are more than a hundred references to Fuhao in the oracle bones of fortune-telling. As the spouse of a Shang king she was involved in state affairs, presiding over rituals, and leading armies in battle. In a series of wars fought by Wu Ding against the neighboring states and tribes, Fuhao was dispatched to recruit soldiers on behalf of the king and was appointed as a general to lead them. She once led 13,000 troops in an attack on the Qiang army, capturing a large number of Qiang soldiers, which made her the general who led the largest number

墟青铜器按用途可分为礼器、乐器、兵器、生产工具、生活用具、艺术品、车马器和杂器等。其中最著名的当数在殷墟王陵区出土的后母戊大方鼎，鼎高133厘米，口长112厘米，口宽79.2厘米，重832.84千克，是目前已知中国古代最重的青铜器。周身以雷纹为地纹，上面又饰以蟠龙纹和兽面纹，造型雄伟，结构复杂，纹饰华丽，铸工精良，表现出很高的技艺水平，堪称此时期的青铜佳作。

后母戊大方鼎、铭文拓片
Houmuwu Rectangular Ding and Its Inscription Rubbing

1976年妇好墓的发掘是安阳殷墟最重要的发现之一。妇好墓虽然没有墓道，墓室不大，但未曾遭过盗掘，保存相当完好，随葬品极为丰富，共出土不同质料的随葬品1928件，有青铜器、玉器、宝石器、象牙器、骨器、蚌器等。妇好是何许人也？为什么在她去世后仍殊荣在身？这可以从殷墟甲骨卜辞中找到答案。甲骨卜辞中有关妇好的记载有一百多条。学者研究认为，妇好是商王武丁的配偶，生前曾参与国家大事，主持祭祀，能征善战，是一名杰出的政治家和军事家，地位显赫。在武丁对周边方国、部族的一系列战争中，妇好多次受命代商王征集兵员，屡任军将征战沙场。她曾统兵1.3万人攻羌方，俘获大批羌人，成为武丁时一次征

of troops in one campaign during the reign of Wu Ding. She also participated in and commanded major operations against the Tu, Ba, Yi and other armies.

468 bronze wares were excavated in the tomb of Fuhao, 190 of which were ritual vessels with inscriptions. Among the 190 ritual vessels, 109 were inscribed "Fuhao", accounting for more than half of the inscribed bronze wares, and most of which were large, heavy vessels and objects of novel and distinctive shape. These groups of bronze ritual objects and weapons are relatively complete as a whole and can thus enhance people's understanding of the ritual system of the time.

The Fuhao bronze wares are of unique shapes and exquisite craftsmanship, which are breathtaking and fully demonstrate the highly developed bronze civilization of the Shang. The Fuhao bronze Double Fangyi (60cm tall, 88.2cm long and 17.5cm wide, now exhibited in the National Museum of China), a miniature of a Shang Dynasty palace, is a rare example of wine vessel in the Shang Dynasty. The Fangyi wine vessel looks like a combination of two, with seven square notches on the long side and seven pointed notches on the other, both designed to hold wine buckets. The lid is sloping on all sides, with a sloping ridge line and a cast-out rib on the center line of the slope, resembling the "si-e" roof style of a Shang palace, with a main ridge and a vertical ridge. The lid ridge has two knobs, facilitating the opening and closing of the lid.

The Double Fangyi is ornately decorated with a cloud and thunder pattern throughout its body, and is carved in relief with animal figures such as beast faces, scops owls, *kui* dragons, and elephants. The inscription of "Fuhao" on the base of the vessel indicates that the vessel was made for Fuhao. We can also see the initial form of a 3000-year-old steam pot in the steam pillar bronze Zhen with the inscription "Hao", which is a rare cooking vessel with a steam pillar in the middle, used to hold food in its belly, placed on a *li*, and steamed by using the rising steam.

Some of the Fuhao bronze wares are in the shapes of birds and other animals, the most famous of which is the "Fuhao" Xiao-shaped bronze wine vessel. The "Fuhao" owl-shaped bronze wine vessel is 45.9cm tall. A pair of these were unearthed. Xiao is a general term for the species of owls in ancient China. The Xiao-shaped bronze wine vessel is shown in the form of a tall, upright Xiao. Like the bird, each Xiao vessel has small ears, a high crown, round eyes, a broad beak, and wings. Three pivot points are formed by its two stout feet and a broad,

战率兵最多的将领，也参加并指挥了对土方、巴方、夷方等重大作战。

妇好墓发掘现场
Excavation Site of Fuhao's Tomb

妇好墓中共出土青铜器468件，有铭文的铜礼器190件，其中铸"妇好"铭文的有109件，占有铭文青铜器的半数以上，且多为大型重器和造型新颖别致的器物。这些青铜礼器、武器组群较为完整，可以增加人们对当时礼制的了解。同时，一些青铜器造型独特、铸工精良，令人叹为观止，充分显示了殷商高度发达的青铜文明。具有商代宫殿缩影之称的"妇好"青铜偶方彝（通高60厘米，口长88.2厘米，口宽17.5厘米，现藏中国国家博物馆），就是商代酒器中的罕见器型。该方彝犹如两个方彝之组合，器身两长边口沿各有七个方形槽和七个尖形槽，是专为放置酒斗设计的。器盖呈四面斜坡状，斜脊线及坡面中线上均铸出扉棱，极似商代宫殿之"四阿"式屋顶，有正脊与垂脊。盖脊有两钮，便于启合彝盖。偶方彝装饰华美，通体以云雷纹做衬地，以浮雕技法表现了兽面、鸱鸮、夔龙、大象等动物形象。器底铭"妇好"二字，表明此器为妇好所作。我们还可以从铭文为"好"的汽柱铜甑形器中看到3000年前的汽锅的雏形，这种中间带汽柱的饪食器较为少见，使用时腹腔盛食

drooping tail. Each vessel is decorated with a neck backed by a hood with a quarter-circle opening behind the head. On the opening is a lid, in front of which there is a standing bird with a dragon behind it. The body of the vessel is ornamented with an elaborate design.

The "Fuhao" Xiao-shaped bronze wine vessel is the earliest bird-shaped bronze treasure ever found in China. The craftsmanship is evidence of a rich imagination which used the animal as an extravagant artistic motif while shaping it into a practical ritual vessel. Moreover, the elaborate ornamentation of the Xiao wine vessel reflected the unique religious sentiments and aesthetic expression of the Shang.

"妇好" 青铜鸮尊
Owl-Shaped Bronze Zun, Excavated from Fuhao's Tomb

Four bronze battle-axes were found in the tomb of Fuhao, one of which weighs 9kg and bears the inscription " 妇 好 ". Shang-era battle-axes could have been used as instruments of torture or for military executions such as the killing of captives after victory in battle. But more commonly, the battle-axe was used as a scepter of power, just as *The Book of History—Muye Oath* states, "in commanding the army, the king holds a yellow battle-axe in his left hand and

物，置于鬲上，利用上腾蒸汽蒸而熟之。

妇好墓中还有一些仿鸟兽形的青铜器，最有名气的当数"妇好"青铜鸮尊。"妇好"青铜鸮尊，属于商代晚期，通高45.9厘米。共出土两件，形制、纹饰、铭文亦基本相近，为一对。鸮是中国古代对猫头鹰一类鸟的统称。鸮尊整体为一昂首挺胸鸮形。鸮小耳高冠，圆眼宽喙，双翅并拢，粗壮的两足与下垂的宽尾构成三个支点。鸮颈后有錾，头部后面开了一个四分之一圆形的口，上面有盖，盖前端有一站立状的鸟，鸟后有一龙。鸮尊器身饰有繁缛纹饰。"妇好"青铜鸮尊是目前中国发现的最早的鸟形铜尊。作器者把丰富的想象与合理的夸张相结合，巧妙地以动物为题材，塑造成实用礼器，既有现实生活的真实写照，又有艺术的概括处理。鸮尊生动的造型、繁缛的纹饰，反映了殷商先民特有的宗教情感和审美观念，是罕见的艺术品。

在妇好墓中发现有4件铜钺，其中一件重达9千克，并带有"妇好"铭文。钺可以作为一种刑具，多用于军旅行刑和作战胜利后斩杀俘虏。钺在古代更多是作为权杖之器，《尚书·牧誓》中有"王左杖黄钺，右秉白旄以麾"，可见，钺乃是兵权的象征。重达9千克的妇好大钺若用于战场，挥动起来未免太消耗体力了，它应是作为仪仗使用的，也正象征了妇好的权势、威仪。

近些年在安阳殷墟发现的重要贵族墓葬中也不乏青铜重器。在一座未被盗掘的武将墓中，共发现随葬品353件，青铜器中作为重器的礼乐器44件，种类齐全，形体较大，花纹繁缛，且多铸有"亚址"铭文。在随葬的青铜器中，兵器232件，占全部青铜器的78%，其中有3件青铜钺，是军事统帅的象征。

商代自盘庚迁殷后，政治稳定，经济随之繁荣，以国都安阳为中心，青铜冶铸业有很大的发展。与商代前期相比，殷墟青铜器不仅数量、种类激增，铸造技术也已十分娴熟。分铸法的熟练应用，使大量精美复杂的青铜器件的铸造成为可能。商代后期的青铜器整体呈现出华美、繁缛、

a white banner in his right hand", showing that the battle-axe was as much a symbol of military power as an instrument of it. The 9kg battle-axe would have been unwieldy in battle. Its function was primarily ceremonial.

In addition to the tomb of Fuhao, other tombs of aristocrats at Anyang Yin Ruins have yielded treasures of bronze. 353 burial objects were extracted from the tomb of a military general. Among these, 44 bronze wares were used as precious ritual and musical instruments. These were of many varieties, large in size, elaborately patterned, and mostly engraved with " 亚址 " inscriptions. Among the bronze objects, 232 pieces of military weapons were found, accounting for 78% of all the bronze findings including three battle-axes.

Bronze smelting and casting had advanced considerably ever since Pan Geng transferred the capital of the Shang to Yin (Anyang) and political stability and economic prosperity had followed. Compared with the early Shang, the quantity, quality, and variety of the bronze objects at the Yin Ruins increased dramatically. Skillful application of the split-casting method made it possible to cast a large number of delicate and complex bronze wares. The bronze objects of the late Shang Dynasty as a whole display an artistic style that is flamboyant, elaborate and mysterious. The mysterious and sacred animal-face motifs, full of strong intimidating power, have been found on all types of bronze wares, and various kinds of three-dimensional shapes of birds and animals and their ornaments are particularly prevalent. The bronze inscriptions that are characteristic of the Shang and Zhou dynasties began to appear and developed from simple to complex, from one or two words to dozens. Bronze art reached its height of splendor in the late Shang Dynasty and continued into the early Western Zhou Dynasty.

The bronze ritual wares at Yin Ruins display a full range of vessels, such as cauldrons, earthenware vessels, *gui*, *li*, beans, jugs, *zun*, *gu*, jars, horns, ampoules, flasks, divorces, *you*, *yi* (sacrificial utensil), *gong* (drinking vessel), *zhi* (drinking vessel), *fou*, buckets, plates, jars, pots, skip-shaped vessels and square vessels, etc. Among these the later types are spoons, *zu* (ancient sacrificial utensil), ladles, *jin* (the base of *zun*), *nao* (ancient musical instrument), etc. Large and square vessels are more prevalent, with thick and solid walls. Among these bronze ritual vessels, wine vessels are the most numerous and varied, which is strong evidence of the extraordinary popularity of drinking among the aristocrats of the Shang Dynasty.

神秘的艺术风格。充满强烈震慑力的诡秘而又神圣的兽面纹，遍饰于各类青铜器，种种像生鸟兽立体造型及其纹饰也格外盛行。商周时代特有的铜器铭纹开始出现，并由简到繁地发展起来，少者一二字，多者数十字。青铜艺术在商代晚期达到了灿烂辉煌的鼎盛时期，并一直延续到西周早期。

殷墟青铜礼器器类齐全，有鼎、甗、簋、鬲、豆、斝、尊、觚、爵、角、瓿、壶、盉、卣、罍、彝、觥、觯、缶、斗、盘、盂、罐、箕形器和方形器，等等。其中新出现的有匕、俎、勺、禁、铙等。大型器、方形器较多出现，器壁厚重，凝重坚实。这些青铜礼器中，酒器不仅数量最多，而且种类繁多，这是商朝贵族饮酒之风异常盛行的有力佐证。根据文献记载，商代的最后一个王——纣王，日夜"沉酗于酒"，后人说他"以酒为池，悬肉为林"。除了贵族外，周人认为商王朝的庶民也过度饮酒。周初的《酒诰》中周公说殷商的庶民群集饮酒，酒腥气味被上天闻到了，上天降下命令灭亡商王朝。西周时期的大盂鼎铭文也有商王朝的诸侯和百官嗜酒，导致商王朝败亡一说。

安阳殷墟出土的青铜乐器主要有铃、铙。20世纪70年代，考古工作者在殷墟西区的M701墓葬中发掘出铜铃14件；妇好墓中出土带铃舌的大小铜铃18件。这类铜铃应为乐铃，通过摇动发出声响，以发挥其多重音响效果。铙是最早使用的青铜打击乐器之一，多三五成组地出土于高级贵族墓葬中。这些成组的编铙形制相同、大小相次，但音阶不全，不能演奏完整的乐曲，应是与其他乐器配合使用的。兵器在青铜器中亦占有很大的比重，有戈、矛、钺、镞、卷头刀、銎斧、头盔等。工具有刀、削、斧、锛、凿、刻刀、锥、锯、钻、钩等。生活用具较少，主要有镜、箸、笄等。

商代后期青铜器纹饰以兽面纹、夔纹和龙纹等幻想动物纹较为常见，且多作为主体纹饰出现。此外，还有鸟纹、蝉纹、蛇纹，以及虎、牛、羊、象等兽纹，云雷纹、三角纹、蕉叶纹、涡纹、目纹等几何形纹。本

According to the historical records, King Zhou, the last king of the Shang Dynasty, "indulged himself in drinking" day and night, and it is said later that "he dumped too much wine into a pool and hung too much meat into a forest", living a corrupt and extravagant life. The people of the successor dynasty, the Zhou, believed that not only the aristocrats but also the common people of the Shang drank excessively. In the early Zhou Dynasty's *Letters of Wine*, the Duke of Zhou said that the common people of the Shang had gathered to drink wine and that the smell had been detected by the heavenly God who then decreed the destruction of the Shang Dynasty. The inscription on a large pellet cauldron from the Western Zhou period also states that the Shang Dynasty's vassals and officials were addicted to wine, leading to the defeat and extinction of the Shang Dynasty.

The bronze music instruments excavated from Yin Ruins in Anyang are mainly bells and cymbals. In the 1970s, archaeologists excavated 14 bronze bells from the burial M701 in the western part of Yin Ruins and 18 large and small bronze bells with tongues were excavated from the tomb of Fuhao. These bronze bells are musical bells, and they produce sounds by shaking so that their multiple acoustic effects could be elaborated. Cymbals were one of the earliest bronze percussion instruments used and were found in groups of three or five in the tombs of senior aristocrats. These groups of cymbals are of the same shapes and of different sizes, but are not fully scaled and cannot play a complete piece of music and were probably used in conjunction with other musical instruments. Military weapons also feature heavily in bronze wares, including dagger-axes, spears, battle-axes, arrowheads, curly-headed swords, axes and helmets. Tools include knives, sharpeners, axes, adzes, chisels, carving knives, awls, saws, drills, hooks, etc. There are fewer household utensils, mainly mirrors, chopsticks and matrices.

Fantastic animal motifs such as animal-face, *kui* and dragon motifs are more common in the late Shang Dynasty bronze wares and are often found as the main motifs. There are also bird, cicada and snake motifs, as well as animal motifs such as tiger, ox, sheep and elephant motifs and some geometric motifs such as cloud and thunder, triangular, palm leaf, vortex and eye motifs. The bronze motifs of this period are featured with three-layer patterns, in which the main motifs such as the cloud and thunder, animal-face and *kui* patterns are protruding on the surface of the bronze vessels, with some shaded lines decorated on the main ones,

时期青铜器纹饰流行三层花纹，即以云雷纹衬地，兽面纹、夔纹等主要纹饰突出于器表之上，主纹饰之上又饰以阴线纹，或者将动物的目部等凸出于主体纹饰之上。这种纹饰繁缛富丽，很有层次感。此外，镂空与镶嵌绿松石的技术也被用于青铜器的装饰。此期铭文内容多是族氏铭文、私名或祖先的人名，字数较少。商代末期出现了较长铭文的青铜器，铭文多达 40 余字。

戍嗣子鼎
Bronze Ding with a Long Text of Inscriptions

殷墟出土的青铜器诡谲神秘的造型、威严凝重的纹饰，反映了殷商先民特有的宗教情感和审美观念，凸显了商王至高无上而充满神秘的统治权威。

3. 河南商代其他青铜器

作为一个奴隶制国家，商王朝自建立之日起就不断对内统治、对外扩张。成汤之时，已是"自彼氐羌，莫敢不来享，莫敢不来王"（《诗经·商颂·殷武》）。盘庚迁殷后，特别是武丁时期，大规模对外用兵，商王朝的疆域有了更进一步的扩展，形成了"邦畿千里，维民所止，肇

or with the eyes of animals protruding on the main motifs. These types of motifs are elaborate and flamboyant, and have a sense of layers. In addition, openwork and turquoise inlay techniques are used in the decoration of bronze wares. The inscriptions of this period are mostly clan inscriptions, personal names or ancestral names, with a small number of Chinese characters. In the late Shang Dynasty, longer inscriptions appeared on bronze wares, with up to 40 characters.

The surreal and mysterious shapes and majestic motifs of the bronze wares excavated at Yin Ruins reflect the unique religious sentiments and aesthetic concepts of the Shang ancestors, highlighting the supreme and mysterious ruling authority of the Shang Dynasty kings.

3. Other Bronze Treasures from the Shang Dynasty in Henan

As a state of slavery, the Shang Dynasty began to rule internally and expand externally constantly from the day it was founded. During the reign of Cheng Tang, the first king of the Shang Dynasty, the state was already one with "no minority states, far and near, dared not come to pay tribute to or worship the king", reflecting the heyday of the dynasty, according to *The Book of Songs*. After Pan Geng's (the 19th king of the Shang Dynasty) transfer of the capital to Yin (the present-day Anyang City), especially during the time of Wu Ding (the 22nd king of the Shang Dynasty), with troops invading the other states on a large scale, the Shang Dynasty expanded its territory much further, and formed a vast empire with "a vast area of territory, and the peaceful and affluent life for its people". Within such a large area, there was a kingdom under the direct authority of the Shang Dynasty, as well as the vassal areas and tribal regions, divided according to their proximity to the dynasty. The Shang culture had a profound influence over a wide and vast area.

The Shang Dynasty expanded its territory through conquest and tributary arrangements. Consequently, Shang bronze culture was diffused over a wider area. Many bronze wares have been found beyond the royal capital in places such as Huixian County, Luoshan County, Wenxian County, Xinzheng and Zhengzhou. These bronze objects all have significant features of the Yin Shang culture in terms of their shapes and ornaments. Huixian County (not far from Anyang and Qixian County) is in a region that is adjacent to the Shang capital. From 1950 to 1952, archaeologists carried out archaeological excavations at Liulige and Chuqiu in

域彼四海"的幅员辽阔的大"帝国"。在这样大的范围内，有归商王朝直接统辖的王畿地区，有根据各地同王朝之间关系的亲疏远近而分成的诸侯地区和方国地区。商文化在广大的区域内，产生了深刻影响。

在商王朝王都之外，如今天的河南辉县、罗山、温县、新郑、郑州等地，也发现有许多青铜器，从这些青铜器的造型和纹饰等方面看，都具有显著的殷商文化的特征。辉县距安阳和淇县不远，属商代的近畿地区。1950年至1952年，考古工作者在辉县琉璃阁、褚邱等地进行考古发掘，发现了商代中、晚期的灰坑、墓葬等重要遗迹。其中墓葬共50余座，这是继安阳殷墟之后在中原地区最早发掘的一群商代墓葬，随葬品有陶、铜、玉石、骨角、蚌器及海贝、金叶等。其中最重要的发现是1952年辉县褚邱出土的一组妇嫀器，共有7件，各器铭文皆同，为"聑斐妇嫀"。铭文所表达的意思是该组器物为"聑斐"族氏所有，为"妇嫀"所用或所铸。该组器物的造型典雅、纹饰精美，被著名古文字学家唐兰先生誉为"稀世珍宝"。据传于20世纪20年代出土于河南辉县的子龙鼎，通高103厘米，口径80厘米，重230千克，体形巨大，造型雄伟。子龙鼎出土后流入日本，2004年日本一位企业家在大阪举办私人收藏品展，子龙鼎在展览中首次露面。2005年底，子龙鼎流入香港，国家文物局与财政部联合开展征集工作，并于2006年4月底，将子龙鼎征集回国。该鼎现由中国国家博物馆收藏。

息国是商王朝偏南的重要方国，处于商文化与荆楚文化的交界地区，从武丁开始，到商王朝灭亡的200多年间，息国贵族一直守卫在南大门。我们从信阳罗山息国贵族墓地的重要发现中，可以了解商代晚期息国的青铜文化面貌。22座商代墓自北而南集中排列在长不过百米、宽不过30米的狭长山坡上。有9座墓共出带"息"字徽识青铜器26件，纹饰风格、制作技法等与安阳殷墟的风格相近，具有商代晚期的风格。这进一步证明，安阳殷墟青铜器对王畿之外一些方国的青铜器产生了重大影响。

Huixian County and discovered some important sites of ash pits and tombs in the middle and late Shang Dynasty. Among them were more than 50 tombs, which were the earliest group of Shang Dynasty tombs excavated in the Central Plains after Anyang Yin Ruins, with burial objects such as pottery, copper, jade, bone horns, mussel wares, sea shells and gold leaves. The most important discoveries of these are a group of Fuchuo wares excavated at Chuqiu in Huixian County in 1952, altogether 7 pieces, with the same inscription "耴斐妇婒". The inscription implies that these wares were owned by the Zhefei clan and were used or cast by Fuchuo. These wares are elegant and exquisitely ornamented. They have been hailed as "rare treasure" by the renowned antiquarian Tang Lan. The Zilong Cauldron, which is said to have been unearthed in the 1920s in Huixian County, Henan Province, is 103cm high, 80cm in diameter and weighs 230kg. It is of great size and majestic form. After its excavation, the Zilong Cauldron found its way to Japan, where it made its first appearance at an exhibition of items from the private collection of a Japanese entrepreneur in Osaka in 2004. At the end of 2005, the cauldron arrived in Hong Kong, where it was obtained by the State Administration of Cultural Heritage in conjunction with the Ministry of Finance and returned to China at the end of April 2006. The cauldron is now in the collection of the National Museum of China.

The Xi State was an important city-state in the southern part of the Shang Dynasty, at the junction of Shang and Jingchu cultures, and was guarded by the Xi State aristocrats for over 200 years from the time of Wu Ding until the end of the Shang Dynasty. The important findings from the burial site of the Xi State aristocrats at Luoshan County in Xinyang provide us insight into the bronze culture of the Xi State in the late Shang Dynasty. Twenty-two tombs of the Shang Dynasty are located from north to south on a narrow slope of fewer than 100 meters long and 30 meters wide. Twenty-six bronze wares with the Chinese character "息" emblem were excavated from nine tombs, and the ornament style and production techniques were similar to those found at Yin Ruins in Anyang, in the style of the late Shang Dynasty. This is further evidence that the bronze wares from the Yin Ruins at Anyang had a major influence on the bronze-making of cities and states beyond the capital.

二、制礼作乐：西周青铜文化

公元前1046年，周武王伐纣，商朝灭亡，统一的周王朝建立，直到公元前771年周王朝被犬戎族所灭，由于这一时期周王居于西方的都城镐京（宗周），因而又被称为西周。西周王朝共历时275年，共传十一代、十二王。西周建立以后，陆续实施了周公营洛、迁移殷民、封建诸侯、制礼作乐等重大举措，奠定了周王朝统治的基础，尤其是以周礼为核心的典章制度及其礼制文化，成为后世文化思想的根基，对中国传统文化影响深远。

西周时期的青铜文化登峰造极，是中国青铜文化发展的鼎盛阶段。西周王朝对归顺的商朝贵族实行了安抚政策，对包括冶铸工人在内的手工业者加以重用，避免了因政权易主造成的生产力重大破坏，这样就保持了包括青铜冶铸在内的手工业生产的继续发展。同时，西周实行的分封政策，也在一定程度上带动和促进了包括青铜铸造业在内的地方经济的发展。

西周时期，铸造青铜器的地点分布更为广泛，中央王朝和诸侯国都城所在地、高等级贵族分封的采邑所在地以及更下一级的区域中心，都发现有青铜冶铸遗址。青铜制品的种类更加丰富，除原来常见的鼎、簋、鬲、甗、爵、觚、觯、罍、盘、盉等，又新增加了镈、钟等乐器，还有镳、衔、节约、马冠、銮铃、辖等车马器。西周时期青铜器的功能更加多样化，礼制化程度进一步加强，青铜器的造型厚重美观，花纹繁缛，还出现了族徽和长篇铭文。这一时期的青铜器不仅涉及当时人们生产、生活的各个方面，还成为统治者维护政治制度和社会稳定的重要工具。

河南地处天下之中、殷商旧地，西周时期的河南地区是姬周文化和殷商文化碰撞、融合、发展，从而形成中国传统文化的最重要的地区。西周初年，周公营建洛邑（成周），用来加强对殷商遗民和东南地区方

II. Rites and Music: The Western Zhou

In 1046 BC, King Wu of the Zhou Dynasty assaulted King Zhou of the Shang Dynasty and brought about the fall of the Shang Dynasty and the founding of the unified Zhou Dynasty, which lasted until 771 BC when the Zhou Dynasty was destroyed by the Quanrong tribes. The Western Zhou was so called because the king of Zhou resided in the capital city of Haojing (also called Zongzhou) which was in the west. The Western Zhou Dynasty lasted 275 years and consisted of eleven generations and twelve kings. After its founding, the Western Zhou Dynasty implemented many significant initiatives such as the establishment of Luoyi (today's Luoyang) as the capital city by the Duke of Zhou (King Wu's brother), the migration of the Shang Yin people, the enfeoffment of vassals, rites making, and music composition, thus laying the foundation of the new dynasty. Crucially, the canonical system and ritual culture (with the Zhou rites as its core) became the foundation of later generations' cultural thought.

Under the Western Zhou, Chinese bronze culture reached its apex. The dynasty pacified the subservient aristocrats of the Shang and elevated the status of craftsmen (including smelting and casting workers) to important positions, avoiding the serious disruption of industry that often accompanies a change of sovereignty. At the same time, the dynasty's policy of enfeoffment facilitated the growth of the local economy including handicrafts such as bronze casting.

During the Western Zhou period, bronze wares were cast over a wider range of locations, with bronze smelting and casting sites found in the locations of the capitals of central dynasties and vassal states, the covens of high-ranking aristocrats, and in regional centers of a lower level. There were larger varieties of bronze wares at the time. In addition to the usual cauldrons, *gui*, *li*, jugs, goblets, dishes and divorces, there were also bronze musical instruments such as *bo* and bells, bronze carriages and horses such as *biao*, *xian*, *jieyue*, horse crowns, bells on royal carriages, and *xia*. During this period, the functions of bronze wares became more diversified and more of them were ritualized, with precious and beautiful shapes, elaborate ornaments and the emergence of clan emblems and long inscriptions. The bronze objects of this period not only covered various aspects of people's daily lives but also functioned as important tools for the rulers

国的统治，洛邑成为与镐京并立的又一王都所在地，也是周王朝统治中国的又一政治、经济、文化中心。西周之初，面对新征服的广大地区，周王采取"封建亲戚，以蕃屏周"的方式巩固自己的统治。分封的对象包括同姓贵族和异姓贵族两类。异姓贵族又可分为功臣谋士、先王圣贤后裔、殷商王族及其他臣服归顺的方国贵族。河南是西周分封诸侯国最多的地区之一，先后有 70 多个诸侯受封于河南。周代的诸侯国初封时规模都不大，国土范围不过方圆百里，这些小国寡民式的封国均有一个特点，就是要筑一座或多座城市作为都邑。所以，古代的都城也可指国，城也称邑。一个封国不仅指城邑，还包括城外的郊、野地区。王亲贵戚和一般士族住在城内，而土著平民多在城外。近 70 多年来，在河南洛阳、鹤壁、鹿邑、三门峡、平顶山等地，相继发现了周王室、卫国、宋国、虢国、应国等西周王室和诸侯国墓地，出土了大量精美的西周青铜器。

1. 洛阳西周王室青铜器

西周王朝建立后，由于洛邑的政治、军事、经济作用，中原和周边地区很快稳定并得以快速发展。西周中期，逐步形成一系列等级森严的典章制度和礼仪规范，主要体现在贵族祭神享祖、礼仪交往、宴飨宾客所使用礼器的数量与规格上，也就是"藏礼于器"。洛阳出土了大批西周王室贵族青铜器，如著名的保尊、保卣、作册大方鼎、令方彝、叔牝方彝、召伯虎盨、王妊簋、太保戈、康伯壶、丰伯剑等，均是西周时期具有代表性的青铜器。这些青铜器的主人，多是史书和文献中屡屡出现的西周王室宗亲与显贵。不仅如此，在洛阳北窑等地还发现了大规模的铸铜作坊遗址，表明洛阳是西周青铜铸造业的中心之一。

洛阳北窑西周早期铸铜作坊遗址，占地达 14 万平方米，是目前全国发现的最大的西周时期青铜冶铸作坊遗址，发现有大、中、小型熔铜炉，大型炉直径 1 米左右，为竖式鼓风炉，炉壁还残留有木炭、铜颗粒和铜渣，炉上发现有残存的鼓风口，表明当时已经用皮囊鼓风，用木炭

to maintain the political system and social stability.

Henan had been the beating heart of the Shang Dynasty and so it was for Western Zhou. By the latter's time, Henan had become the engine that produced and refined traditional Chinese culture, where the cultures of Ji Zhou and Yin Shang collided, merged and developed. In the early years of the Western Zhou Dynasty, Zhou Gong built Luoyi (also called Chengzhou) to strengthen his rule over the remnants of the Yin Shang Dynasty and the states of tribes in the southeastern region. Luoyi became another royal seat alongside Haojing, and China's another political, economic and cultural center ruled by the Zhou Dynasty. At the beginning of the Western Zhou Dynasty, the king adopted the method of "enfeoffing the relatives and meritorious officials, and allowing them to establish their states to protect the Western Zhou Dynasty" to consolidate the Western Zhou over the vast newly conquered areas. The enfeoffed subjects included aristocrats of the royal family and aristocrats outside the family. The aristocrats outside the royal family included the meritorious officials and resourceful scholars, descendants of former kings and sages, the royal families of the Shang Dynasty, and other subservient aristocrats from the states of tribes. Henan was one of the regions with the largest number of enfeoffed states in the Western Zhou Dynasty, with over 70 vassals enfeoffed in succession. These vassal states were all of small sizes at the very beginning, covering over 30 miles in circumference, and one feature of all these small enfeoffed states was that one or more cities had to be built to serve as capitals. Therefore, in ancient times, a capital city could be a state, and a city was also called Yi. An enfeoffed state was not only a city, but also included the suburbs and wilderness outside the city. The king's relatives and the general aristocrats lived within the city, while the indigenous commoners lived mostly outside the city. In the last 70 years or so, in Luoyang, Hebi, Luyi, Sanmenxia and Pingdingshan, tombs of the Western Zhou royal family and vassal states such as the Zhou royal family, the Wei State, the Song State, the Guo State and the Ying State have been discovered, and a large number of exquisite Western Zhou bronze wares have been unearthed.

1. Bronze Treasures of the Western Zhou Royal Families from Luoyang

After the founding of the Western Zhou Dynasty, the political, military,

做燃料，采用内加热的方法熔化铜液铸造青铜器。这些熔铜炉已经具备近代鼓风炉的雏形，说明当时的冶铸技术已有较高的水平。铸铜作坊遗址还出土大量陶范，主要有鼎、尊、觚、爵等青铜器范。外范分为内外两层，每块外范都有榫眼、榫卯和长方形子母口，陶范制作精细，保证了青铜铸件的精美。铸造程序是先铸好大型器物的附件，然后嵌入整个铸器的外范，再用铜液浇注，使其合成一体。

洛阳北窑一带还发现有西周贵族墓地，出土了大量的青铜礼器、兵器、生产工具、车马器和杂器，表明西周青铜铸造在数量、品种上有了更大的发展，而且制作十分精美。特别是兽面纹方鼎、方座簋和母鼓方罍三件青铜重器，造型古朴庄重，花纹繁缛精细，为西周青铜制品中的佳作，代表了当时青铜铸造工艺的最高水平。虽然当时普遍采用浑铸法，但器物上的浮雕兽头采用了分铸法铸造，说明当时已能熟练采用规范统一的范型，而且已经开始使用焊接修补技术。这一时期还能够根据器物本身的用途，采用最适合的合金成分比例，大大提高了青铜产品的质量。

洛阳出土的保尊
Bronze Bao Zun, Excavated in Luoyang

and economic role of Luoyi led to the rapid stabilization and development of the Central Plains and surrounding areas. In the middle of the Western Zhou Dynasty, a series of hierarchical rules and ritual norms gradually emerged, mainly in terms of the number and specifications of the ritual vessels used by the aristocrats in worshipping their gods and ancestors, in ceremonial interactions, and in feasting guests, which was also called "hiding rites in vessels". A large number of bronze wares of the Western Zhou aristocrats were excavated in Luoyang. The well-known bronze objects such as Baozun wine cups, Baoyou wine wares, Zuocefangding wine wares, Lingfangyi wine wares, Shupinfangyi wine wares, Zaobohuxu food wares, Wangrengui wine wares, Taibaoge weapons, Kangbo kettles and Fengbo swords were all representative in the Western Zhou period. The owners of these bronze wares were mostly royal family members and dignitaries who appeared frequently in historical books and documents. In addition, large-scale bronze casting workshop sites were found in places such as the Luoyang North Kiln, indicating that Luoyang was one of the Western Zhou bronze casting centers.

The early Western Zhou bronze casting workshop site at the Luoyang North Kiln, covering an area of 140,000 square meters, is the largest bronze smelting and casting workshop site of the Western Zhou period ever found in China. There were large, medium, and small copper melting furnaces of which the large ones were about one meter in diameter and were vertical blast furnaces with charcoal, copper particles, and copper slag still remaining on the inner walls and with residual blast outlet found on the furnaces. This suggests that the bronze objects were already cast by using leather pouch blowers, using charcoal as fuel, and by using the internal heating method to melt the bronze liquid. These bronze furnaces had the embryonic forms of modern blast furnaces, suggesting that smelting and casting technology at the time was already of a high level. At the bronze casting workshop site, a large number of pottery moulds mainly of caudrons, *zun*, goblets and jars for bronze wares have been excavated. Each outer mould included two layers, with a mortise, a tenon, and rectangular kit ports. The pottery moulds are finely crafted to ensure the exquisite quality of the bronze castings. The casting procedure is to cast the accessories of the large wares first, embed the outer mould of the entire casting wares, and then pour in the bronze

洛阳出土的叔牝方彝
Bronze Fang Yi, Excavated in Luoyang

2. 河南西周殷系青铜器

周武王在推翻商王朝统治后,首先做的就是安抚商民、册继殷祀、表彰商贤。周成王时期还将大量殷顽民迁至洛邑,目的就是加强对殷遗民的统治,彻底断灭他们的复国梦想。周王朝的这些政策,使商代社会的旧有结构和文化传统得以保存,也让商代青铜文化在河南地区顽强地延伸。在河南出土的西周早期青铜器中,殷商风格的青铜器占很大比重,而且在称谓、干支记名、族徽、器型等诸多方面继承了商代传统,显然是殷遗民所作。

在洛阳北窑村就有数处聚族而葬的西周初年殷人墓,从中发现了不少带有殷商遗风的青铜器。这些器物的主人,多是归顺周王室的殷商旧臣,他们在西周初年对于商周文化的融合、礼仪典章制度的建立起了很大的作用。

1997年在鹿邑县太清宫发现的西周长子口墓,是极为少见的周初

liquid to make them melt into one piece.

A large number of bronze ritual wares, military weapons, production tools, carriage and horse wares, and miscellaneous items have been unearthed at the Luoyang North Kilns. This indicates that bronze casting in the Western Zhou period developed further in quantity and variety, and was more exquisite than in earlier periods. In particular, the three precious bronze vessels, including the beast-faced square cauldron, the square-seated *gui* and the Mugu square fang *lei* with their simple, dignified shapes and elaborate ornaments, are the best of the Western Zhou bronze products, representing the highest level of bronze casting craftsmanship at the time. Although the mixed casting method was commonly used at the time, the relief animal heads on the bronze vessels were cast using a separate casting method. This indicates that the standardized and unified moulds were already used proficiently, and that the welding repair techniques were already put into use. In the Western Zhou period, according to the practical use of the bronze wares, people could adopt the most appropriate alloy composition ratio that greatly improved the quality of the bronze products.

洛阳出土的王妊簋
Bronze Gui, Excavated in Luoyang

2. Bronze Treasures of the Yin Series in the Western Zhou Dynasty, Henan

Following the overthrow of the Shang Dynasty, the first thing that King Wu of the Zhou Dynasty did was to pacify the Shang people, enshrine the Yin sacrifices and honour the Shang sages. During the reign of King Cheng of the

殷遗民大墓。这座大墓有两条墓道，墓内殉祭 14 个人牲，墓底中部有殉人与狗的腰坑，这是商代葬俗的完整保留。研究成果显示，墓主人很可能是归顺周王朝后被册封为宋国之君的微子启。长子口墓随葬了大批极富商文化特色的青铜器，展现了一代诸侯国君的气派。其中青铜礼乐器达 85 件，仅带有铭文的就有 50 多件，多数自铭为"长子口"，出土器物种类丰富。其中青铜礼乐器的组合，特别是酒器的组合，与殷墟晚商墓葬的组合相同。

鹿邑太清宫长子口墓出土的扁足鼎
Bronze Ding with Flat Feet, Excavated from Changzikou's Tomb, Luyi

鹿邑太清宫长子口墓出土的簋形觥
Gui-shaped Bronze Gong, Excavated from Changzikou's Tomb, Luyi

Zhou Dynasty, a large number of Yin recalcitrants were transferred to Luoyi, with the aim of strengthening the rule over the Yin remnants and completely extinguishing their dreams of restoration. These policies of the Zhou Dynasty preserved the old structures and cultural traditions of the Shang society and allowed the continuation of Shang bronze culture throughout Henan. Among the early Western Zhou bronze wares unearthed in Henan, those in the Yin Shang style account for a large proportion, and they inherited many aspects of the Shang tradition, including appellations, the nomenclature by using heavenly stems and terrestrial branches, clan emblems and vessel shapes. These wares were the work of the Yin remnants.

In the North Kilns Village of Luoyang, there are several tombs of the early Western Zhou period where the Yin people of the same ethnic groups were buried, from which a number of bronze wares in the style of the Yin Shang have been found. Most owners of these bronze wares were the former officials of the Shang Dynasty who had surrendered to the Zhou royal family. These officials played an important role in the integration of the Shang and Zhou cultures and the establishment of the ritual and regulatory systems in the early years of the Western Zhou period.

The Shang and the Western Zhou practiced human and animal sacrifice. The Changzikou tomb of the Western Zhou Dynasty, discovered in 1997 at Taiqinggong in Luyi County, Henan Province, is an extremely rare large tomb of the Yin people in the early years of the dynasty. It features two burial paths, 14 human sacrificial remains, and a waist pit for human and dog martyrdom in the middle of the tomb floor. Research has shown that the owner of the tomb is likely to have been Weizi Qi, who was enthroned as the king of the Song State after his surrendering to the Zhou Dynasty. The Changzikou tomb contains a large number of bronze vessels with detailed Shang-inspired characteristics, showing the grandeur of a vassal ruler. Among them are 85 bronze ritual and musical instruments, more than 50 of which bear inscriptions, mostly inscribed "长子口", and rich varieties of bronze vessels. The combination of bronze ritual and musical instruments, especially of wine vessels, is identical to that found in the late Shang tombs at Yin Ruins.

1999 年，在郑州市西北的洼刘遗址发现了一批西周贵族和平民墓葬，出土了大量西周早期的青铜礼器、兵器和车马器，许多青铜器还带有族徽和铭文。目前公开发掘信息的 M1 墓葬级别最高，随葬品也最为丰富。该墓墓室长 3.5 米，宽 2.2 米，墓底四周有二层台，葬具为一棺一椁。随葬的青铜礼器 12 件，包括鼎 3 件，扁体卣 2 件，尊、簋、甗、罍、觚、盉、圆体卣各 1 件，其中 10 件铸有铭文，如"举父丁"鼎、"史父辛"鼎、"亚其父乙"鼎、"车"罍、"其父辛"盉、"目父亥"簋等。这批青铜器的组合、形制和纹饰，既有商代的遗韵，又有西周早期的创新，是商周文化融合的产物。

1986 年在信阳浉河港的河道淤泥中发现了 14 件青铜器，推测原属墓葬随葬品。这批器物造型优美，制作精湛，为同期青铜器中罕见的珍品。根据形制和铭文特征，这批青铜器明显分为"父乙""父丁"两组。其中"父乙"组铜器 10 件，包括簋、卣、觚各 1 件，角、尊各 2 件，此外还有卣盖、觚盖、勺各 1 件。"父丁"组铜器 4 件，包括簋 2 件，卣、觯各 1 件。从形制和纹饰来看，这些青铜器中的簋、尊等器与陕西宝鸡等地出土的西周早期同类器接近，应同属西周早期铜器群。两组铜器在形制风格和铭文特征上较为一致，应是出自同一座或两座墓葬。这两组青铜器的器类多属酒器，是典型的殷商作风。铭文中还出现有商人称谓和族徽，说明

信阳浉河港出土的兽形觥盖首
Lid to the Animal-Shaped Bronze Gong, Excavated at Shihegang, Xinyang

鹿邑太清宫长子口墓出土的方斝
Bronze Fang Jia, Excavated from Changzikou's Tomb, Luyi

In 1999, several tombs belonging to Western Zhou aristocrats and commoners were found at the site of Waliu, northwest of Zhengzhou. A large number of the early Western Zhou bronze ritual objects, military weapons, and carriage and horse wares were unearthed, many with clan emblems and inscriptions. The tomb M1, which makes its excavation information public, is the most bountiful of all the burial places uncovered to date. Its chamber is 3.5 meters long and 2.2 meters wide. It features a two-storey platform rising from its base with an inner and outer coffin.

Twelve bronze ritual objects were buried in the tomb, including three cauldrons, two flat-bodied wine containers, and a *zun*, a *gui*, an earthenware, a goblet, a divorce, and a round-bodied wine container. Ten of these are cast with inscriptions, such as the "举父丁" cauldron, "史父辛" cauldron, "亚其父乙" cauldron, "车" earthenware, "其父辛" divorce, and "目父亥" *gui*. The combination, form, and ornamentation of these bronze objects are products of the fusion of the Shang and Zhou cultures, with a mixture of Shang beauty and early Western Zhou innovations.

这批器物与西周初年封国的殷商贵族有关。

信阳浉河港出土的"父乙"铜卣

Bronze Fuyi You, Excavated at Shihegang, Xinyang

1951年鲁山仓头发现西周初年青铜器5件，1956年上蔡田庄出土西周早期青铜器7件，这些器物从组合和形制上都带有浓重的晚商遗风。其中鲁山青铜尊铭文为"子孙父庚"，上蔡青铜瓿铭文为"作父辛尊亚矣"，不仅器型风格接近，且都有着晚商器铭常见的记铭方式。

1976年在襄县霍庄村发掘的西周墓葬，其结构形式仍继承殷商传统，在墓底中部设殉狗腰坑，墓内随葬青铜容器7件，包括鼎、簋、卣、尊、觯各1件，爵2件。在出土的"矢父辛"组铜器中，酒器占多数，青铜尊铭文为"忧矢乍父辛宝彝"。这种以酒器为主的组合和卣、爵形制带有明显的晚商风格，而鼎、簋、尊的形制和铭文已有西周早期的新风格。这些西周早期青铜器，多为商周交替时，殷人流迁南下在豫南鄂北所留下的痕迹。

In 1986, fourteen bronze wares were discovered in the river sludge at Shihe Harbor, Xinyang, presumably as burial objects. They are beautifully shaped, superbly crafted, and are rare treasures. Based on their form and inscriptional design, they can be neatly divided into two groups: "Fu B" and "Fu D". The "Fu B" group consists of one *gui*, one wine container, a goblet, two horns, two *zun*, one wine container lid, one goblet lid, and one spoon. The "Fu D" group consists of two *gui*, one wine container, and one goblet. The *gui* and *zun* wares are close to their early Western Zhou counterparts excavated in Baoji, Shaanxi, and are supposed to have belonged to that dynasty as well. The two groups are supposed to come from the same one or two tombs. They are mostly wine vessels in the style of the Yin Shang. Furthermore, the merchant appellations and clan emblems in the inscriptions suggest that the wares were associated with the Yin Shang aristocrats of the early Western Zhou fiefdom.

信阳浉河港出土的"晨肇贮"角
Bronze Chenzhaozhu Jiao, Excavated at Shihegang, Xinyang

In 1951, five bronze wares of the early Western Zhou were brought to light at Cangtou in Lushan and in 1956 another seven at Tianzhuang in Shangcai. All of these bear a strong late-Shang influence. The bronze *zun* from Lushan is inscribed

3. 浚县辛村卫国贵族墓地青铜器

周公平定殷商故土的叛乱后，册封其同母弟弟康叔于卫地。卫国成为护卫周王室的重要支柱和屏障，其封地在殷墟及其周围数百里的地方，大体包括今河南北部和河北南部地区。卫国以其特殊的地理位置，成为护卫周王室的重要支柱和屏障，也担负着镇压、监视和管理殷墟附近殷遗民的重任。周厉王之前，卫国的历史少见记述。春秋初年，卫庄公即位后，卫国虽仍为东方大国，但已经开始衰退了，内忧外患不断，先后迁居于曹地（河南滑县东）、楚丘（河南浚县东）、帝丘（河南濮阳）等地。战国时期，卫国加速衰败，夹在赵、魏、齐、楚、秦之间苟延残喘，朝秦暮楚。秦二世元年（公元前209年），卫国国君角被废为庶人，卫国灭亡，是最后灭亡的周朝封国。

考古发掘证明，今河南淇县、浚县一带，是西周时期卫国的中心。1932年至1933年，原中央研究院会同河南对浚县辛村卫国墓地进行发掘，共发掘墓葬82座，分大、中、小三型墓。在严重盗掘的随葬残余中，仍有珍贵的器物出土。出土的甲泡上有"卫师易"之铭，据此可推断这里是卫国贵族墓地。从中型墓M60出土的青铜尊上的铭文可知墓主人

鹤壁庞村出土的"鱼父己"卣（附枓）
Bronze Yufuji You, Unearthed from Pang Village, Hebi City (and Dou)

with "子孙父庚", while the bronze goblets from Shangcai are inscribed with "作父辛尊亚矣". These are not only close in form, but are similar to late-Shang inscriptions.

The structure of the Western Zhou tombs excavated in 1976 in Huozhuang Village, Xiangxian County, bear the inheritance of the Yin Shang Dynasty, with a waist pit in the middle of the base and seven bronze vessels buried inside the tomb including a tripod, a *gui*, a wine container, a *zun*, a goblet, and two jars. Among the "矢父辛" group of bronze vessels excavated, wine vessels are the main ones, and the bronze *zun* is inscribed with "忧矢乍父辛宝彝". This grouping with wine vessels as the main products, and the forms of wine containers and jars have a distinct style of the late Shang Dynasty, while the form and inscriptions of the cauldrons, *gui* and *zun* bear the new style from the early Western Zhou period. These bronze wares of the early Western Zhou period are mostly traces of the migration of the Yin people southwards to northern Henan and Hubei at the turn of the Shang and Zhou dynasties.

3. Bronze Treasures Unearthed from the Noble Tombs of the Wei State at Xin Village, Xun County

After putting down the rebellion of the Shang Dynasty, the king of the Zhou Dynasty conferred his young brother the title of Kangshu in the territory named Wei, i.e. the Wei State. The State became an important power in the defense of the Zhou Dynasty. The territory of Kangshu belonged to the Yin Ruins and its surrounding areas included the northern part of Henan and the southern part of Hebei. The Wei State featured by its special geography became the pillars for supporting the Zhou royal family and played the role of governing the citizens of the Shang around the Yin Ruins. Before King Li of the Zhou Dynasty, the history of the Wei State was rarely recorded. By the beginning of the Spring and Autumn Period, the Wei State was wracked with internal and external fights and wars and began to decline although Wei was still the big oriental state. The Wei State successively had to move to Caodi(now in the east of Hua County, Henan Province), Chuqiu (now in the east of Xun County, Henan Province), Diqiu (now in Puyang City, Henan Province) and other places. In the Warring States Period the Wei State accelerated to decline, which existed in trouble among the

是一从卫国到西周宗周就职的殷商遗民陆姓贵族。青铜车马器中的人面铜饰、兽面铜饰、包金车饰，都是稀世珍品。离辛村墓地不远的鹤壁庞村西周墓，也是西周早期卫国贵族墓葬，出土的"冉父乙"觯、"鱼父己"卣等青铜器形制和纹饰也表现出浓厚的殷商遗风。

4. 三门峡虢国墓地青铜器

虢国是周代姬姓国，虢国国君在两周之际为朝廷重臣，曾随周平王东迁，辅佐周王室。西周至春秋时期，共有五个虢国，后人以西虢、东虢、南虢、北虢、小虢区别。三门峡则为西虢东迁的立国之地，国中有上阳、下阳之分，亦称南北二虢。西周时，西虢为周王室往来东西都城的必经之地，周王从洛邑西归镐京时，必定要经过虢国，周厉王时的虢公长父、周宣王时的虢文公，以及春秋早期的虢公忌父，均为周王室卿士，权重一时。

1956年至1958年，黄河水库考古队在三门峡库区清理了234座墓葬、3座车马坑和1座马坑，出土各类文物9197件，其中青铜器181件。1990年，河南省文物考古研究所在上次发掘的北部，又发现一处贵族墓地，发现九鼎墓2座、七鼎墓1座、五鼎墓1座、三鼎墓1座，分别对应2位国君、1位太子、1位大夫和1位姬妃，出土了大批珍贵的文物，品类包括铜、铁、金、玉、石、陶、竹木、皮革、麻布等。由此，时隔30多年的两次考古发掘，揭开了虢国神秘的面纱。

三门峡虢国墓地是一处等级齐备、布局完整的两周时期大型邦国公墓。其中2001号墓陪葬大型车马，出土各类文物3200多件，其中青铜器170多件，带铭文的就有35件，其中青铜鼎铭文曰"虢季作宝鼎季氏其万年子子孙孙永宝用享"。此墓中出土的玉柄铁剑，是迄今发现的时代最早的人工冶铁的实物，它将中国冶铁历史提前了近200年。还有玉瞑目、联璜组玉佩、金腰带饰等珍贵文物，都为考古史上所罕见。继此墓之后的2009号大墓，是目前所发现的虢国墓地中形制最大、规格

Zhao State, the Wei (魏, sharing the same sound, but a different state), the Qi State, the Chu State and the Qin State. In 209 BC the king of the Wei State was demoted to the ordinary person, and the State was destroyed, which was the last destroyed state of the Zhou Dynasty.

Archaeological excavations have approximated the center of Wei to have straddled Qi and Xun counties. From 1932 to 1933, the former Academia Sinica excavated the Wei cemetery in Xin Village, Xun County, in conjunction with Henan archaeologists. A total of 82 tombs were excavated, which were divided into large, medium, and small. Among the remains, a nail bubble bears the inscription "Weishiyi", from which it can be inferred that this was the cemetery of the nobles of Wei. From the bronze inscription unearthed from the medium-sized tomb M60, it can be seen that the owner of the tomb was a noble named Lu. The bronze accessories to the carriages include ornaments in the shapes of human and animal faces and gold-clad cars. Bronze vessels such as the vessel with the inscription of "Yufuji" unearthed from the tomb of the Western Zhou Dynasty in Pang Village, Hebi City, also showed a strong inheritance of Yin and Shang design.

4. The Bronze Treasures Unearthed from the Tombs of the Guo State in Sanmenxia City

From the Western Zhou Dynasty to the Spring and Autumn Period, there successively existed the Western Guo State, the Eastern Guo State, the Southern

鹤壁庞村出土的"白"簋

Bronze Bai Gui, Unearthed from Pang Village, Hebi City

最高的九鼎大墓，墓中出土的丰富繁多的各类器物中，各式青铜礼乐器200多件，大多铸有"虢仲"铭文，其中各式乐器就有4套之多。虢国墓地出土的青铜列鼎中的圜腹蹄足，与西周晚期王室形制一致，青铜乐器甬钟不仅在形制上为西周晚期之典型器，而且其音位的排列也保持了西周以来无商音的四声结构。三门峡虢国墓地排列有序的墓葬、保存完整的葬式、典型的器物的组合，为研究两周之际虢国的宗法、族葬、礼制、经济等多方面内容提供了坚实的物证。

根据目前的研究成果，上村岭虢国墓地2009号墓的主人应该是辅佐周厉王的虢公长父，2001号墓主人虢季是周宣王时谏王不籍千亩的虢文公。2000年至2001年，三门峡李家窑城址发掘工作揭露了大面积的城垣与城壕、宫城与环壕，还有制陶、制骨、冶铜手工业作坊，以及粮库等遗迹，使得虢国都城上阳城的布局和内涵更加清晰。这些大型宫殿性建筑基址及遗存，年代在西周晚期至春秋中期。因此，上阳城将与虢国墓地一起，成为人们认识虢国的更有力依据。

三门峡虢国墓地出土的"虢季"鬲

Bronze "Guoji" Li, Unearthed from the Tomb of the Guo State in Sanmenxia

Guo State, the Northern Guo State and the Small Guo State. The Western Guo State moved to Sanmenxia City (Henan Province) to build its capital. The Western Guo State was divided into the nothern part and the southern part, which developed separately into the Northern Guo State and the Southern Guo State. In the Western Zhou Dynasty, the Western Guo was vital for the Zhou royal family to travel between the east and the west. When the king of Zhou returned from Luoyi to Haojing, he must pass through the Guo State. The kings of the Guo State successively took the important positions in the Zhou Dynasty.

From 1956 to 1958, the Yellow River Reservoir archaeological team cleared 234 tombs, 3 carriage pits, and 1 horse pit in Sanmenxia reservoir area, and unearthed 9,179 pieces of various cultural artifacts, including 181 bronze vessels. In 1990, Henan Institute of Cultural Artifact and Archaeology discovered another noble cemetery in its northern part. 2 Jiuding tombs, 1 Qiding tomb, 1 Wuding tomb and 1 Sanding tomb were found that separately belonged to two kings, a prince, a minister and a concubine. A large number of precious cultural artifacts were unearthed including copper, iron, gold, jade, stone, pottery, and bamboo. So the two archaeological findings through more than 30 years provide more knowledge of the Guo State.

The cemetery of the Guo State in Sanmenxia is a large one with complete grades and layout in Zhou Dynasty fashion. In Tomb No. 2001 large carriages and more than 3,200 pieces of various cultural relics were unearthed including more than 170 bronze vessels and 35 pieces with inscriptions. The jade-handled iron sword unearthed in this tomb is the earliest physical object of artificial iron smelting discovered thus far in China. Tomb No. 2009 is the Jiuding Tomb with the largest shape and the highest specification found in the cemetery of Guo. Among its various artifacts, there are more than 200 bronze ritual instruments, most of which are cast with the inscription "Guozhong"; among these are as many as 4 sets of various instruments. The bronze cauldrons with a round belly and beast feet unearthed in Guo's cemetery are consistent with the shape of the royal family in the late Western Zhou. Chimes, the bronze musical instruments, were typical in the late Western Zhou Dynasty in shape, and had the same tones like those in the Western Zhou Dynasty. The ordered tombs, well-preserved burial styles, and the combination and characteristics of the utensils in the cemetery of

三门峡虢国墓地出土的"虢季"铜列鼎
"Guoji" Bronze Ding, Unearthed from the Tomb of the Guo State in Sanmenxia

三门峡虢国墓地出土的"丰白"簠
Bronze "Fengbai" Fu, Unearthed from the Tomb of the Guo State in Sanmenxia

Guo in Sanmenxia provide solid material evidence for the patriarchal clan system, clan burial, ritual system, economy, and other aspects of the Guo State in the Western Zhou Dynasty and the Eastern Zhou Dynasty.

The current research shows that the owner of Tomb No. 2009 in Shangcunling of Guo was most likely a king of Guo who assisted King Li of Zhou, and that the owner of Tomb No. 2001 is Guoji who made suggestions to King Xuan of Zhou. The unearthed objects of the two tombs are also in the style of the late Western Zhou Dynasty. From 2000 to 2001, the excavation of Lijiayao City Site in Sanmenxia exposed a large area of city walls and trenches, as well as relics of pottery making, bone making, copper smelting handicraft workshops, grain depots and such which vividly depicted the layout and connotation of Shangyang City, the capital of Guo. The base sites and remains of these large-scale palace buildings date from the late Western Zhou Dynasty to the mid-Spring and Autumn Period. Therefore, Shangyangcheng together with the Guo cemetery, will become a powerful basis for people to know more about Guo.

5. 平顶山应国墓地青铜器

应国是商周时期河南地区的古老封国，在商代就已存在，西周初年，周武王之子又加封于此，公元前7世纪时被楚国所灭。应国的封地在今平顶山市一带。1986年至1996年，河南省文物考古研究所对应国墓地进行了连续10余年的发掘。应国墓地主要是周代应国贵族的埋葬地，其中也包括应国灭亡后部分楚国贵族墓葬与两汉时期的一些平民墓。应国墓地共发掘应国墓葬80多座，排列有序，其中有应公墓及应公夫人墓、应侯墓，出土西周早期到春秋早期的大量青铜器。

墓地中出土的柞伯簋造型奇特，底部设一喇叭形支座，用以垫高器身。簋内底部铸有铭文，共8行74字。记录了西周初年在王室举行的一次射礼活动的全过程。柞伯因射出的10支箭均中了靶的，获得了冠军，周王就把10块红铜赐给他，并且又赐给他2件乐器。柞伯用这些铜材制作了这件珍贵的用来祭祀周公的铜簋。这篇优秀的叙事铭文为研究中国古代射礼制度提供了十分珍贵的资料。射礼是先秦礼乐文明的重要组成部分，是指集射箭、礼教和娱乐于一体的弓矢竞技活动，在西周时期演变为周天子维护统治的手段，也是周天子观察各级贵族美好德行、选拔人才的重要渠道。

在一些小型墓葬中，也出土有精美的铜器，比如M50墓葬中的"匍"雁形盉，盉整体似一雁，以雁颈为盉流，雁尾有一龙形鋬，尾上附一牛首，牛首上立一人，高髻长衫，腰束革带，双手抱盖环，将器盖与器身巧妙相连，造型新奇。盖内有40余字铭文，记述了盉的主人"匍"作为应国的使者，赴邢国探访邢国国君邢公，并用邢公所赐的铜制作了这件盉以作纪念。

5. Bronze Treasures Unearthed from the Cemetery of the Ying State in Pingdingshan

The Ying State was an ancient vassal state in Henan during the Shang and Zhou dynasties, which had existed since the Shang Dynasty. In the early Western Zhou Dynasty, King Wu of Zhou granted his forth son the title and land in this state, which covered Xuezhuang Village, Pingdingshan City today. This state was destroyed by the Chu State in the 7th century BC. From 1986 to 1996, Henan Institute of Cultural Relics and Archaeology had excavated the cemeteries of the Ying State. These cemeteries consist of mainly the burial places of the nobles of the Ying State, some of the nobles of the Chu State, and some of the common people in the Han Dynasty. More than 80 tombs of the Ying State were excavated. The cemeteries of the king, queen, and lord were laid out in an orderly fashion. From these cemeteries of Ying, a large number of bronze wares from the early Western Zhou Dynasty to the early Spring and Autumn Period had been unearthed.

Zhabo Gui, one of these bronze wares, was made in distinguished form with a trumpet-shaped pedestal to support the ware body. The inscription found in the bottom inside its body includes 74 Chinese characters in 8 lines, which record a shooting competition among the royal family in the early year of the Western Zhou Dynasty. Zhabo was the champion as he shot 10 arrows in the target, so the

柞伯簋
Bronze Zhabo Gui

"匍"盉
Bronze He

在激烈的兼并战争中,诸侯国之间为了政治的需要,在战争中常用政治联盟和联姻外交策略。应国墓葬出土的铜礼器中,有不少器物的铭文记载了应国与周边诸侯国互通婚姻的史实。M45 墓葬为春秋早期应国贵族墓,出土有一大批青铜礼器,不少铸有铭文。据鼎铭"应申姜作宝鼎,其子子孙孙永宝用",可知墓主人为嫁到应国的申国女子。此外,先后发现的 4 件邓公簋,铭文内容为"邓公作应嫚毗媵簋,其永宝用",表明系邓公嫁女于应国所作媵器。应国与申、邓等国联姻的媵器的发现,反映了当时应国与申、邓等周边诸侯国的友好关系。

应国墓地所出土铜器的铭文涉及大射礼、俯聘礼、帝王庙号、丧服制度,对古代礼仪制度与诸侯方国史研究有重要价值。已发掘的西周初年应国大型墓葬,带有明显的商人遗风,特别是在青铜器的组合上,爵、卣、尊、觯等青铜酒器类占了相当大的比例,说明商文化在殷商故地的生命力。西周晚期的应国大型贵族墓如 M1,出土器物中青铜礼器、车马器齐全,并有大量玉器,随葬五鼎的青铜器组合符合墓主人作为邦国

king gave him 10 pieces of red bronze and 2 musical instruments as the reward. Later Zhabo had made the valuable bronze vessel for sacrifice of the king with the bronze. The excellent inscription provides the important material for the study of Chinese ancient shooting activities and rules. The shooting activity is the necessary part of ritual and music civilization before the Qin Dynasty, which covered the shootings, ritual activities and amusements. The kind of activity had gradually developed into the means by which the king of the Zhou Dynasty maintained his authority, in which the king observed the characters and behaviors of the nobles, and selected the talent people.

In some small cemetries, the fine bronzes also have been unearthed. A creeping-goose-shaped he was unearthed in a cemetry marked M50 by the archaeologists. This bronze like a goose in a whole has a spout as the neck of a goose and a dragon-shaped handle in the tail of a goose, where a man stands straight on the cattle head with a topknot of hair, long garment, leather belt in the waist, and a pot lid in hands. This design linked the lid and the body skillfully. Inside the lid there are 40 characters which describe Pu, the master of the bronze worked as the envoy of the Ying State to visit the king of the Xing State and made this bronze by the gift given by the king of Xing.

In the fierce annexation wars, the political alliance and marriage diplomacy were often used among vassal states for political needs. Among the bronze ritual vessels unearthed from tombs of the Ying State, there are many inscriptions carved in these vessels that record the historical stories about the marriages between the Ying State and its neighbour states. In a noble tomb of Ying in the early Spring and Autumn Period, a large number of bronze ritual vessels were unearthed, many of which were cast with inscriptions. According to the inscription "Shenjiang of Ying had made this *ding*, and her sons and grandsons can inherit it for ever", we can know that the master of this tomb was a woman of the Shen State married to the king of the Ying State. Besides the bronze, 4 Denggong *gui* had been unearthed successively with the inscription "Denggong had made this vessel because his daughter Man Pi was married to the Ying State" which shows Denggong married his daughter to Ying. The vessels with inscriptions about the marriages among the Shen State, the Deng State and the Ying State reflect the peaceful relations between Ying and its neighbour states.

大夫的身份。

侧面人像
Silhouette of the Human-face Bronze

6. 其他西周诸侯国青铜器

此外，在河南的淮阳、信阳、南阳等地，也发现了不少西周诸侯国的青铜器。1973年以来，淮阳曾连续发现了陈国贵族青铜器。2012年在南阳市东北的夏响铺村，发现了西周鄂国贵族墓20多座，其中有鄂伯或鄂侯及其配偶的墓葬，部分青铜器上铸有"鄂侯夫人"铭文。

7. 西周时期青铜器特点和用鼎制度

河南地区出土的西周青铜器的数量超过商代，制作也更加精美。西周早期青铜器继承了商代的华丽繁缛，除器物的个别部位出现新的元素外，几乎与商代青铜器如出一辙。酒器在青铜器组合中占比较大，青铜器的形制、主体纹饰，以及铭文书体、标识族徽的习惯等方面，都保持

The inscriptions on the bronze wares excavated from Ying cemeteries described the imperial ritual, engagement ritual, titles of kings after their death, and the mourning apparel system, which are of great value to the study of the ancient etiquette system and the history of vassal states. The large tombs of Ying had obviously the style of the Shang Dynasty, especially in the combination of bronze vessels. Bronze wine vessels such as *jue*, *you*, *zun*, and *fu* account for a considerable proportion, and their characteristics show the continuity of Shang influence. The large aristocratic tomb M1 contained numerous bronze vessels including accessories of carriages, a large number of jade articles, and especially the combination of five *ding* which symbolizes the status of the tomb owner.

6. Bronze Treasures Unearthed from Tombs of the Lords in the Western Zhou Dynasty

Bronze vessels of the Western Zhou era have been found in Huaiyang, Xinyang, Nanyang and other places in Henan Province. Since 1973, many wares of the nobles of the Chen State have been found in several locations in Huaiyang. In 2012, in Xiaxiangpu Village, northeast of Nanyang City, more than 20 tombs of the nobles of the E State in the Western Zhou Dynasty were discovered, including the tombs of Marquis E Bo and his wife where some bronze vessels were cast with the inscription "Mrs. Marquis E Bo".

7. The Rules of Ding and the Characters of Bronze Treasures in the Western Zhou Dynasty

The bronze wares unearthed in Henan Province in the Western Zhou Dynasty exceed those of the Shang Dynasty not only in number, but also in production. Bronze objects in the early Western Zhou Dynasty adopted the splendor of those in the Shang Dynasty, and they were almost the same as those of Shang except for some new factors in some parts of the utensils. Wine vessels account for a large proportion in the bronze wares. The shape, ornamentation, inscription, and the use of the family emblem maintained the continuity of the late Shang. After the middle period of the Western Zhou Dynasty, the ritual and music system as well as regime of the rulers of the Zhou Dynasty reached maturity. Zhou bronze vessels from this period began to depart from the Shang

了商代晚期的风格。西周中期以后，统治者的礼乐制度和政权建构走向完善与成熟，青铜器的制作与礼制的实施结合得更为密切。中期以后的青铜器，纹饰与形制摆脱了晚商的影响，纹饰删繁就简，新出现许多纹饰，盛行鸟纹，流行变形的夔纹、窃曲纹、环带纹、重环纹、瓦纹、垂鳞纹；铭文字数增多，多长篇铭文，在书体和行文上更加规范，多数是册封和追孝彰德之意。

西周时期，青铜礼器开始有了定制，器类变化很大，更加注重青铜食器的组合；方形青铜鼎消失不见，方座青铜簋和合口盖簋取代了商代旧制，青铜簠、盨开始出现，酒器中青铜爵、觚、斝基本上见不到，到西周晚期时完全绝迹。青铜方壶、圆壶和编钟开始出现。除了食器和酒器，乐器在周代也进入了大发展的时期，周人将音乐、舞蹈、诗歌纳入规范社会等级的制度中，形成周代的"礼乐制度"，青铜乐器作为最重要的乐器在重大场合演奏，与石质乐器一起构成"金石之音"，包括钟、镈等。这些乐器按音阶序列与大小成套出现，数量多、体量大，往往需要悬挂在架上演奏，又被称为编钟、编镈等。在祭祀或宴饮时，鼎中盛放着肉食，巨大的编钟被有节奏地敲响，这便是钟鸣鼎食。

西周还改变了商人以觚、爵酒器区分等级的传统，开始采用鼎、簋等食器为核心的礼器组合，其他还包含酒器、水器等青铜器类别，而其重心则是青铜鼎，所以礼器所反映的等级制度又被称为用鼎制度。根据目前所掌握的资料，商代用鼎制度尚不明朗，到西周时期，开始形成了严格的用鼎制度。根据文献记载，西周时期用鼎制度大致可分为五等，各等人用鼎的数量皆与其身份和地位相适应。这五等人及其用鼎数量分别是：天子九鼎，诸侯七鼎，卿大夫五鼎，士三鼎，庶人一鼎。这五等之间界限森严，不可逾越，如有逾越，则受惩罚。春秋时期，周王室衰微，诸侯国逐渐崛起，用鼎制度开始出现僭越现象，即下等的人用上一等人的用鼎数目，这是礼崩乐坏的一种表现，已得到考古学资料的印证。

heritage and established their own aesthetic. They became more closely associated with the rites of the Zhou Dynasty. The Western Zhou bronze vessels were simplified, and many new patterns were designed, such as bird pattern, *kui* pattern, stealing curve pattern, ring pattern and so on. The words in bronze inscriptions had increased and many long inscriptions became standardized, most of which were about conferring titles and paying homage to their master.

In the Western Zhou Dynasty, bronze ritual vessels began to be customized, and the types of vessels changed greatly, with emphasis on the characteristics of the combination of bronze utensils. The square bronze tripod had not been popular, while the square bronze *gui* and the closed *gui* replaced their counterparts of the Shang Dynasty, and *fu* and *xu* began to be popular. The bronze wine vessels such as *jue*, *gu* and *jia* were completely not in use in the late Western Zhou Dynasty. Bronze square pots, round pots and chimes began to be used. Apart from food and wine vessels, the Zhou Dynasty broke new ground in the innovation of musical instruments. Musical instruments also entered a period of great development in the Zhou Dynasty, and the Zhou people incorporated music, dance and poetry into the system of standardizing social classes. From then on the ritual and music system of the Zhou Dynasty gradually formed. Bronze instruments such as bells and *bo* played an important role on important occasions, and cooperated with stone instruments to form the "music of bronze and stone". These musical instruments appear in complete sets according to the scale sequence and size. They are numerous and bulky, so they often were hung on a rack to play. They are also called chimes and cymbals. When offering sacrifices or feasts, the meat was put in the tripod, and the huge chimes were sounded rhythmically. This is the famous occasion where the people can enjoy meat in tripod with the ring of bells.

Instead of the tradition of symbolizing social grade of the Shang Dynasty with wine vessels, the Zhou Dynasty adopted the combination of ritual vessels mainly with *ding* and *gui*, sometimes bronze vessels such as wine vessels and water vessels mainly with bronze *ding*. Therefore, the social grade system represented by ritual vessels was also that of bronze *ding*. According to the available information, how to use *ding* in the Shang Dynasty was still vague, and by the Western Zhou Dynasty the system of how to use *ding* became stricter. Under the Zhou, the

在用鼎制度中，与鼎搭配使用的是另一种礼器——青铜簋。簋用来盛放黍稷稻粱等食物，在周代祀典和宴乐中，常以偶数出现，与奇数的青铜列鼎配套使用。据礼书所载，其制度是：九鼎配八簋，七鼎配六簋，五鼎配四簋，三鼎配二簋，一鼎无簋。

ding system was roughly divided into five classes, and the number of *ding* used represented their identity and status. Nine *ding* for the emperor, seven for the vassal, five for the minister, three for the scholar official and one for the common people. The boundaries among these five grades were so strict and insurmountable that if they were overstepped, the offender would be punished. The ritual vessel *gui* was associated with the *ding* system. Gui was used to hold food such as broomcorn millet, millet, rice, and sorghum. It was often used in even numbers in sacrificial rites and feasts. Odd numbers were for bronze tripods. According to the ritual books, nine *ding* with eight *gui*, seven with six, five with four, three with two, and one *ding* without *gui*.

三、中原逐鹿：东周青铜文化

公元前771年，周平王东迁洛邑，自此开始了中国历史上的东周时期，直至公元前256年为秦所灭。东周分为两个阶段，从周平王东迁（公元前771年）到周敬王四十四年（公元前476年）称春秋时期；从周元王元年（公元前475年）到秦王嬴政二十六年（公元前221年）秦朝建立称战国时期。东周时期的河南，除周王畿外，最多时有50多个诸侯国，春秋时期有郑、卫、宋、陈、蔡等国，战国时期有韩、魏、卫及楚国的部分疆土，是列国逐鹿争霸的大战场。当西周结束，东周开始，"礼崩乐坏"的时代便开始了，这个时期，周王室已不再具有西周时期那样支配其他诸侯国的统治地位，诸侯们纷纷无视礼制，比如春秋五霸之一的楚庄王，公然向周王室询问代表王权的九鼎轻重，是为问鼎中原。

东周时期是中国青铜文化的又一个高峰，也是中国青铜时代的绝唱。与前期不同的是，东周青铜器铸造不再是集中于周王室，而是分散到各诸侯国家，形成地区性艺术特色，尤其是楚国、郑国等国，它们的青铜器铸造水平远远超过了周王室，达到了一个新的高度。这时的青铜器被广泛用于诸侯国家和贵族之间的礼聘、馈赠、贿赂、交换、抵押等交际活动。各地诸侯与贵族的需求，促使青铜器的铸造技术再次升级，过去青铜器统一的规范被打破，各地青铜器无论造型还是纹饰都呈现出了强烈的地域风格。新的器类、奇特的造型层出不穷，艺术家的创造才能得到了前所未有的发挥，特别明显地反映在一些人和动物形象的造型设计上。东周青铜器逐渐摆脱了作为宗法等级和礼乐制度的物化形式的束缚，脱离了商代恐怖神秘和西周庄严凝重的礼制规范，表现出日益生活实用化的趋势，开始越来越多地进入人们的日常生活领域，透射出以人为本的光泽，成为秦汉以后青铜器完全世俗化发展的先声。

东周青铜器的器类，既有祭祀宴飨或婚丧礼仪时使用的礼器和乐器，

III. Fighting for Supremacy in the Central Plains: The Eastern Zhou

In 771 BC, King Ping of the Zhou Dynasty moved to Luoyi. This turn of events inaugurated the Eastern Zhou Dynasty, a new phase in Chinese history. The Eastern Zhou Dynasty was divided into two period. The first is the Spring and Autumn Period (771-476 BC), and the second is the Warring States Period (475-221 BC) and ended with the establishment of the Qin Empire. During the Eastern Zhou Dynasty, in Henan there were more than 50 vassal states, except King Ji of the Zhou Dynasty. Separately in the Spring and Autumn Period there were the Zheng State, the Wei State, the Song State, the Chen State, the Cai State and others, and in the Warring States Period there were the Han State, the Wei (魏 in Chinese) State, the Wei State (卫 in Chinese) and the Chu State. They fought in Henan, the central plains for supremacy. As we've seen with the end of rites and music in the death throes of the Western Zhou, the royal family no longer held the dominant position over the vassal states and their former power was not to be revived under the Eastern Zhou. The vassals had grown accustomed to ignoring the court and doing anything they wished within their respective realms. The King Zhuang of the Chu State even openly asked the royal family of Zhou about the weight of Jiuding representing the kingship, which suggested that he wanted to be the King in the Central Plains.

In the Eastern Zhou Dynasty Chinese bronze culture reached another peak. The collapse of royal power led to a flowering of creative expression and this was reflected in bronze art. The upshot was that bronze casting was no longer the exclusive privilege of the royal family. Vassal states began producing their own bronze objects and this led to regional artistic variations, especially in Chu and Zheng, whose bronze casting far surpassed that of the royal family of the Zhou Dynasty. During this time, bronze objects were widely used in courtship and exchanged as gifts, bribes, and mortgages between vassals and nobles. The breaking of the Zhou Dynasty's monopoly on bronze casting created a boom in demand. Unified standards were abandoned and as regional varieties proliferated, new instruments and a variety of shapes emerged in an endless stream. Improvements

也有车器、马饰、兵器、工具及生活用具。商代和西周盛行的酒器大量减少,青铜尊、觚、爵、觥、斝、觯、卣、彝等器类逐渐被淘汰。青铜鼎和簋作为礼器常以单、偶数相配套的形式使用,烹饪器和食器数量增多,出现了青铜盆、炉、敦、鉴、缶等新型器物。除了沿袭西周时期的甬钟和镈钟外,还有钮钟、钲、錞于等青铜乐器问世。镜、灯、奁、带钩、带扣等生活用品逐渐增多。随着商品生产和交换的发展,青铜货币开始广泛使用,各国都在使用本国的货币,如布币、刀币、圆钱、铜贝等。由于东周时期战争频发,尤其盛行车战,因此青铜车马器更加发达,新出现了殳、弩等武器装备,青铜兵器制作也更加精良。同时还出现了传递军令的青铜虎符和证明身份地位的青铜玺印,以及用于度量衡的青铜砝码、量、尺等青铜工具。东周时期的青铜器造型由厚重威严变得奇巧轻灵,浓厚的神秘色彩渐渐消退,纹饰开始变得更接近生活,已极少使用商代和西周时期那种宗教色彩浓郁的兽面纹,代之而起的是日趋生活化的动物纹、植物纹、几何纹、人物纹等,素面器也开始盛行,长篇铭文已不多见。

东周时期河南地区的青铜铸造业高度发达,战国时期的梁(今开封)、宁(今获嘉)、共(今辉县)、郑(今新郑)、新城(今伊川西南)、阳人(今汝州西北),都是当时制造青铜兵器和钱币的冶铸中心。多年来,在今河南境内发现了多处东周时期的重要青铜冶铸遗址和最具代表性的诸侯国青铜器群之一。

1. 洛阳东周王室青铜器

东周时期的洛阳作为天子之都,在星罗棋布的列国都邑中,仍保持着宗主国的躯壳,是当时规格最高的都城。从周平王东迁至周景王时,洛阳东周王城经历了周王室12世共250多年。这里出土的青铜器数量巨大,集中分布在东周王城及东周王陵区。早在20世纪上半叶,洛阳金村王陵区就出土了众多极为精美的青铜器,震惊了世人。这些青铜器

were made in the modeling of human and animal images. Bronze ware in the Eastern Zhou Dynasty eventually broke the bonds of the clan, ritual, and music regime. It also left behind the horror and mystery of the Shang Dynasty and the solemn and dignified ritual norms of the Western Zhou Dynasty. Bronze began to enter people's daily lives, a harbinger of the complete secularization and popularization of bronze culture after the Qin and Han empires.

Bronze wares in the Eastern Zhou Dynasty include ritual and musical instruments used in sacrificial banquets or weddings and funerals, as well as chariots, accessories to carriage, weapons, tools, and daily necessities. The number of popular wine vessels in the Shang and Western Zhou dynasties decreased and bronze objects such as *zun*, *gu*, *jue*, *gong*, *jia*, *zhi*, *you* and *yi* were gradually eliminated. As ritual vessels, the bronze *ding* in odd number and *gui* in even number are often used together. The number of cookers and food utensils had increased, and new utensils such as bronze pots, stoves, bowls, mirrors and *fou* became popular. In addition to metal chimes and *bo* in the Western Zhou Dynasty, bronze musical instruments *niuzhong*, *zheng* and *chunyu* came out. Mirrors, lamps, caskets, hooks, buckles and other household utensils were gradually increasing. With the development of commodity production and exchange, bronze coins were widely used, and all states were using their own currencies in the forms of cloth coins, knife coins, round coins and copper shells. Due to the frequent wars in the Eastern Zhou Dynasty, especially the carriage wars, bronze chariots were more developed, new weapons and equipment such as crossbows appeared, and bronze weapons were more sophisticated. Bronze *hufu* was used to convey military orders, bronze seals represented the power and social position, and bronze weights, scales and rulers for weights and measures also began to be used. In the Eastern Zhou Dynasty, the bronze had been smart and light. Those bronze objects with mystery gradually were abandoned, and the bronze ornamented with daily things became popular. The mysterious animal face patterns in the Shang Dynasty and the Western Zhou Dynasty were rarely used in bronze, and the bronze objects with the new animal patterns, plant patterns, geometric patterns, and figure patterns as well as plain-faced utensils became popular. Bronze vessels with long inscriptions were rare.

During the Eastern Zhou Dynasty, the bronze casting industry in Henan

除铸有各种精美的蟠螭纹外,还出现了人与虎、豹、鹿等兽搏斗场面的狩猎纹图案,特别是错金银青铜器的大量发现及浑铸、焊接、熔铸等工艺的运用,标志着东周时期的青铜铸造仍处在一个比较发达的阶段。如1929年洛阳东郊金村大墓出土的错金银鎏金狩猎纹铜镜,直径达17.5厘米,就是一件独一无二的集鎏金、错金银工艺于一身的周王室生活用器。

洛阳东郊金村大墓出土的错金银鎏金狩猎纹铜镜
Bronze Mirror, Inlaid with Gold and Silver with the Hunting Pattern, Excavated from the Tomb of Jincun Village, Luoyang City

近年来对东周王城的发掘有了新的进展。继20世纪50年代洛阳中州路出土260座东周墓葬后的半个多世纪中,洛阳东周王城内又陆续发现一批"甲"字形贵族大墓及陪葬殉马坑。出土青铜器的时代跨度从春秋早期到战国晚期,相当于周平王东迁到秦统一的整个东周时期。其中一件在洛阳东周王城陵区出土的战国错金银铜鼎,虽然造型小巧,但纹饰图案对称工整,装饰华丽,显得精巧玲珑,堪称国之瑰宝。2001年在洛阳二七中学发现了目前东周王陵内唯一的一座带有四条墓道的大墓,由于被多次盗掘,仅出土了爵、斝、鼎等青铜器,铜鼎上有"王作宝尊彝"铭文,从墓葬规格和铭文分析,这座大墓应该是东周某一位周王的墓。

reached new heights. During the Warring States Period, Liang (now Kaifeng), Ning (now Huojia) and Gong (now Huixian), Zheng (now Xinzheng), Xincheng (now southwest of Yichuan) and Yangren (now northwest of Ruzhou) were the casting centers for manufacturing bronze weapons and coins at that time. Over the years, many important bronze smelting and casting sites in the Eastern Zhou Dynasty and the most representative bronze groups of vassal states in China have been found in present-day Henan.

1. Bronze Treasures Unearthed from the Imperial Tombs of the Eastern Zhou Dynasty in Luoyang

Luoyang, as the capital of the Eastern Zhou Dynasty, remained the hub of the dynasty among all the states. Luoyang witnessed the development of the dynasty for more than 250 years and a large number of bronze vessels have been unearthed from the tombs of the Eastern Zhou Dynasty. In the first half of the 20th century, many extremely exquisite bronze vessels were found in the imperial tombs of Jincun Village, attracting worldwide attention. These bronze vessels are cast with exquisite *panchi* patterns, hunting patterns in the fighting scenes between humans, tigers, leopards, deer and other beasts. In particular, the discovery of a large number of gold and silver-rubbed bronze vessels and the application of techniques such as mud casting, welding, and melt casting indicate that bronze casting in the Eastern Zhou Dynasty reached a relatively developed stage. For example, in 1929, the gold and silver-rubbed bronze mirror with hunting patterns unearthed from the tomb of Jincun Village in the eastern suburb of Luoyang, with a diameter of 17.5cm, is a unique household vessel of the Zhou royal family.

In recent years, new progress has been made in the excavations in Luoyang. More than half a century after 260 tombs of the Eastern Zhou Dynasty were unearthed in Zhongzhou Road in the 1950s, a number of "甲"-shaped noble tombs and carriage pits have been found as well. The unearthed bronze vessels span from the early Spring and Autumn Period to the late Warring States Period. Among them the gold-silver rubbed bronze and copper *ding* of the Warring States Period is exquisite, although it is small with symmetrical and neat patterns and gorgeous decorations. In 2001, in Erqi Middle School of Luoyang the tomb

洛阳东郊金村大墓出土的人物立像
Bronze of a Standing Man, Unearthed from the Tomb of Jincun Village, Luoyang City

2. 郑国青铜器

公元前 806 年，周宣王的弟弟受封于郑（今陕西渭南市华州区东），是为郑桓公。西周末年，周王室危机四伏，北方戎狄猖獗，郑桓公身为司徒，预感到周王朝的衰败，采纳了太史伯的建议，提前东迁到虢、郐两国之间（今河南荥阳、新郑一带），先后灭掉郐与东虢。西周亡国后，郑桓公之子郑武公护驾周王东迁有功，继为周王室卿士，在原虢、郐故地重建郑国，定都于新郑。今河南新郑市区的郑韩故城即其都邑遗址。郑庄公时，郑国势力不断发展强大，四处攻伐。在与周桓王率领的周、陈、蔡、卫诸国联军的征战中，郑庄公大破王师并射伤周桓王，成为春秋初年不可一世的小霸主。后来郑国内乱不断，又因地处交通要塞，春

of the Eastern Zhou Dynasty which was a unique one with four ways was found. The tomb had been robbed many times, so only bronze wares such as *jue*, *jia* and *ding* remained and they bore the inscription "王作宝尊彝". According to the tomb specifications and inscriptions, this tomb likely belonged to a king of the Zhou Dynasty.

洛阳东周王城陵区出土的错金银铜鼎

Bronze Ding, Inlaid with Gold and Silver, Unearthed from the Tomb of Jincun Village, Luoyang City

2. The Bronze Treasures of the Zheng State

In 806 BC, King Xuan of the Zhou Dynasty awarded the land to his younger brother in Fengxiang, Shaanxi Province. His young brother was then named King Huan of the Zheng State. At the end of the Western Zhou Dynasty, the royal family was in crisis, and the Rongdi State was rampant in the north. The King Huan of Zheng foresaw the decline of the Zhou Dynasty, and adopted the suggestion of Taishibo to move eastward to the area between the Guo State and the Kuai State (now Xingyang and Xinzheng in Henan Province) in advance, and destroyed Kuai and Eastern Guo successively. After the subjugation of the Western Zhou Dynasty, King Wu, the son of King Huan, contributed a lot in moving capital, so he was promoted. He rebuilt Zheng in the old places of the Guo State and the Kuai State, and made its capital in Xinzheng. Today, the old city of Zhenghan in Xinzheng, Henan Province is the site of its capital. In the

秋时期一直是大国争夺的中心，国势发展受挫。虽然春秋末期子产执政时，郑国一度受到晋楚强国的尊重，但是弱国地位难改。战国时期，郑国国内君臣争权，外受韩国蚕食，终于在公元前375年被韩国所灭。

中原的郑国，地处东周列国频繁的交往、会盟、征战、婚媾、商贸等之中心，经济文化先进，民人富足多识，春秋一世，郑国文化在礼乐上挑战传统，开辟了东周列国文化的崭新面貌。

郑韩故城是春秋战国时的著名都城，郑、韩两国先后在此建都长达530年之久。城内发现多处贵族墓地及铸铜、铸铁、制骨遗址。郑国铸铜遗址面积达10万平方米，发现大量的铜渣、木炭屑、陶范碎片、鼓风管等。熔炉炉底呈圜底状，炉壁外抹有一层草拌泥以聚热保持炉温，说明当时已采用了鼓风助燃技术。从出土陶范看，主要生产镬、铲、镰、锛、凿等青铜工具。

20世纪以来，郑韩故城出土了大量精美的青铜器。1923年，郑韩故城西城南部李家楼以出土莲鹤方壶等百余件春秋时期青铜重器而举世闻名，这些青铜器当时被称为"新郑彝器"，其中青铜礼器有鼎、簋、鬲、方甗、簠、罍、方壶、圆壶、盘、匜、鉴、炉、舟、编钟等，食器、酒器、水器、乐器齐全，其中莲鹤方壶又被视作当时社会变革的象征和新时代的标志。1993年以来，在郑韩故城的东城，发现了多座青铜礼乐器窖藏坑和大量车马坑。多座青铜礼乐器坑和大批青铜礼乐器的发现，填补了周代社祀（周人通常把祭祀土地神的场所称为"社"）礼制形式的空白，对于研究当时祭礼的用鼎、用牲和与之有关的仪礼运作方式等有重要意义。特别是九鼎八簋的礼器组合打破了周礼的规制，表现了东周时期礼崩乐坏的社会现象。

新郑郑国青铜器有着面目一新的新颖风格，虽然在器物组合方面仍然具有很强的礼制特色，但许多器物的造型和花纹风格与以往判然有别。如带盖的青铜鼎、雕镂精细的蟠螭纹和夔凤纹等，均为前所未有的新形式。特别是像莲鹤方壶这样工艺精湛、具有不朽艺术生命力的作品，集

ruling period of King Zhuang of Zheng, Zheng grew stronger to attack other states. In the battle with the allied forces of Zhou, Chen, Cai and Wei, led by King Huan of Zhou, King Zhuang defeated the states and killed King Huan, then the Zheng State became the great state in the early Spring and Autumn Period. Later, due to the civil wars, as well as its important location, Zheng was fought for by other big states in the Spring and Autumn Period which stopped its development. Although Zheng was once respected by the big states, i.e. Jin and Chu, Zheng which became weak was hard to exist. During the Warring States Period, Zheng was taken up by the Han State in 375 BC.

The Zheng State in the Central Plains was located in the center of frequent exchanges, alliances, wars, marriages, commerce in the Eastern Zhou Dynasty. Its economy and culture were advanced, and its people were rich and knowledgeable. In the Spring and Autumn Period, the culture of Zheng was different from those traditional rites and music, which opened up a new culture of the states in the Eastern Zhou Dynasty.

The ancient city of Zheng and Han was a famous capital in the Spring and Autumn and the Warring States periods, when Zheng and Han successively established their capitals for 530 years. Many noble cemeteries and sites of copper casting, iron casting, and bone making were found in the city. The copper site in Zheng covered an area of 100,000 square meters, where a large number of copper slag, charcoal scraps, pottery fragments, and blast pipes have been found. The bottom of the furnace is round and outward, and a layer of grass mixed with mud is smeared on the outside of the furnace wall to collect heat to keep the furnace temperature. This indicates that blast combustion-supporting technology was adopted at that time. The presence of a pottery mold suggests bronze tools such as shovels, sickles, spears and chisels were produced here.

Since the 20th century, a large number of exquisite bronze wares have been excavated in the old city of Zheng and Han. In 1923, Lijialou in the south of Xicheng, the old city of Zheng and Han, was world-famous for yielding more than 100 pieces of heavy bronze wares from the Spring and Autumn Period, among which the famous bronze is Lotus and Crane Square Pot. At that time, they were called "Xinzhengyi ware". The bronze ritual wares were *ding*, *gui*, *li*, square pot, round pot, plate; besides there are many food vessels, wine vessels,

中体现了春秋中期以后苛求创新和变革的精神。春秋时期，郑国长期在晋、楚两个大国的夹缝中求生存，朝晋暮楚。莲鹤方壶的造型和纹饰也表现出了多元文化融合的特征，器型与西周晚期方壶近似，莲瓣也是从西周时期青铜器的立体环带纹饰演变而来，显然是接受了传统周文化的影响；壶顶的立鹤，明显是受到晋文化青铜器鸟形顶饰的影响；龙形耳的装饰及怪兽形足又具有楚文化的浪漫主义特征。春秋时期是中国历史上新旧思潮交替、社会急剧变革的时期。作为时代产物的莲鹤方壶，打破了旧有的传统，个性张扬释放，开启了一代先风，因此，郭沫若先生曾称莲鹤方壶为"时代精神之象征"。

1923年郑韩故城郑公大墓出土的莲鹤方壶
Bronze Rectangular Hu with Lotus and Crane Patterns, Unearthed from the Tomb of the King of the Zheng State in the Old City of Zheng and Han in 1923

water vessels and music instruments. Since 1993, a number of bronze ritual instrument pits and a large number of carriage pits have been found in the east side of the old city of Zheng and Han. The excavation of a number of bronze ritual instruments pits proved the existence of the ritual form of social sacrifice in the Zhou Dynasty, which was of great significance to study the use of *ding*, sacrifice and the related rituals at that time. Especially, the combination of rites and utensils in Nine Ding and Eight Gui broke the rules of Zhou, which showed the collapse of rituals in the Eastern Zhou Dynasty.

The bronze wares of Zheng in Xinzheng bore a new style. Although they retained strong ritual characteristics in the combination of utensils, the shapes and patterns are different from those of the past. For example, the bronze tripod with a cover, the finely carved *panchi* pattern, and phoenix pattern are all unprecedented new forms. In particular, the bronze vessels show exquisite craftsmanship and immortal artistic vitality, such as the Lotus Crane Square Pot, and embody the spirit of innovation and change that characterized the years after the mid-Spring and Autumn Period. During the Spring and Autumn Period, Zheng had to struggle for its existence between the Jin State and the Chu State

郑国公举行大典的祭祀坑：新郑郑国祭祀遗址 15 号坑
The Sacrifice Pit for the Imperial Ceremony Hosted by King Guo of the Zheng State:
No.15 in Site of Sacrifice of Zheng in Xinzheng

郑韩故城出土的九鼎八簋
Bronze Set of the Nine-Ding-Eight-Gui System, Unearthed from the Old City of Zheng and Han

3. 辉县琉璃阁卫国墓地青铜器

周武王将其子康叔分封到殷商故地，是为卫国。进入春秋以后，卫国内外交困，国势日衰。在齐、晋与戎狄势力交互胁迫下，国都一再迁徙，春秋时期卫国的邦国墓地成为一个历史之谜。自1936年以来，属于卫国域内的辉县一带，发现多处殷商至东汉时期的贵族墓地。其中琉璃阁东周墓地是一处邦国的族群墓葬，而且主墓与从葬的墓葬分布有序，很可能就是卫国的公室墓地。琉璃阁墓地内出土的青铜器品类丰富，传统与创新并存，反映出中原卫国的历史与文化进程。

1936年，河南博物馆在辉县琉璃阁墓地的东北角发掘了甲、乙两座大墓，出土了大量精美的青铜器。琉璃阁墓地所出土的青铜器，有许多与新郑铜器纹饰相近之处。在器物配置上，琉璃阁墓地与春秋中期中原一带诸侯墓的鼎制一致，其中甲墓有列鼎7件、陪鼎9件、镬鼎1件，应是属于诸侯一级大墓。辉县甲、乙二墓青铜器部分保留了西周末期到春秋早期的风格，同时又具备了春秋晚期到战国初期的新器型。

both of which were bigger. The shape and ornamentation of the pots also show the characteristics of multicultural integration. Its shape is similar to that of the square pot in the late Western Zhou Dynasty, and the lotus petal evolved from the three-dimensional girdle ornamentation of bronze wares of the Western Zhou Dynasty, accepting the influence of the Zhou culture. The crane on the top of the pot is influenced by the bird-shaped top decoration of bronze vessels in the Jin culture; The decoration of dragon-shaped ears and monster-shaped feet also has the romantic characteristics of the Chu culture. In the Spring and Autumn Period the new thoughts naturally replaced the old and the society changed rapidly. Lotus Crane Square Pot showed its attractiveness, which symbolized the pioneering spirit. Therefore, Mr. Guo Moruo once said the pot was the symbol of the spirit of the times.

3. Bronze Treasures Unearthed from Tombs of the Wei State in Liulige, Huixian County

King Wu of the Zhou Dynasty granted his son named Kangshu the old city of the Shang Dynasty, which was the Wei State. Since the Spring and Autumn Period, the domestic and foreign affairs of Wei was tough which suggested the declining of Wei. Under the coercion of the Qi State, the Jin State and the Rongdi State, the capital of Wei was moved many times, so the cemetery of Wei

辉县琉璃阁出土的龙耳铜罍

Bronze Lei with Dragon Handles, Unearthed in Liulige, Huixian County

辉县琉璃阁出土的龙兽纹四耳鉴

Bronze Jian with Dragon and Animal Patterns, Unearthed in Liulige, Huixian County

4. 河南楚国青铜器

楚国建立于西周初年，从春秋时期开始，楚人一直致力于北上中原，原来属于周文化范围的汉淮流域各诸侯国，都在楚人北上过程中，归附于楚而最终为其所灭。楚灭国数十，拓地千里，陈兵周郊，问鼎中原，是当时南方最强大的国家，并表现出称霸中原的雄心。战国初年，秦国

in the Spring and Autumn Period was a historical mystery. Since 1936, many noble cemeteries from the Shang Dynasty to the Eastern Han Dynasty have been found in Huixian County, which belonged to the territory of Wei. Among them, Liulige cemetery of Eastern Zhou is an ethnic tomb, and the main tomb and the subordinate tombs are distributed in an orderly manner, which is probably the royal cemetery of Wei. The bronze vessels unearthed in Liulige demonstrated that tradition and innovation in some cases coexisted, reflecting the history and culture of the Wei State in the Central Plains.

In 1936, Henan Provincial Museum excavated two tombs, namely tomb A and tomb B in the northeast corner of Liulige cemetery in Huixian County, and discovered a large number of exquisite bronze wares, including 7 Lie *ding*, 9 Pei *ding* and 1 Huo *ding*. According to the *ding* system of the Zhou Dynasty, the owner of the tomb should have been a vassal king. Both tombs retain the style from the Western Zhou Dynasty to the early Spring and Autumn Period, and at the same time, they introduced new bronze types from the late Spring and Autumn Period to the early Warring States Period.

辉县琉璃阁出土的镶红铜龙纹扁壶

Bronze Hu with Dragon Patterns, Unearthed in Liulige, Huixian County

将领白起攻打楚国，楚顷襄王退至陈城（今淮阳），国势日衰，最终为秦所灭。

楚文化分布的地域，在今湖南、湖北、河南、安徽四省。河南是楚文化策源和发展的重要区域，楚人曾多次将他们辉煌的史诗篇章留在中原大地上。据统计，河南已发掘的楚墓就有 200 座以上，其中以信阳长台关、淅川下寺、信阳楚王城、淮阳陈楚墓地等为代表。淅川下寺出土的王子午鼎、王孙诰编钟、云纹铜禁、镶嵌绿松石神兽等更是楚国青铜器乃至中国青铜器的翘楚，显示出楚国青铜器铸造技术的高超水平。

20 世纪 70 年代以来，在河南淅川发现了多处楚国贵族墓地，尤其是 1978 年至 1979 年淅川下寺楚墓群和 1990 年至 1991 年淅川和尚岭、徐家岭楚墓群两次重要的考古发掘，为世人所关注。在出土的众多青铜器中，以礼乐器最为引人注目，这些器物不仅器型高大，纹饰瑰丽，且铸工精湛，许多器物上都有铭文。淅川楚墓青铜器群以灵动华丽的造型风格、纤密的蟠螭与蟠虺纹构成韵律感极强的主体纹饰等，显示了楚人丰富浪漫的想象力和鲜活的生命力。其中 1978 年淅川下寺楚墓群出土的王子午鼎，共有 7 件，形制相同而大小相次，整组铜鼎造型雄伟，制作精良，装饰繁缛，精细华美，多处使用了焊接工艺。这组铜鼎无论是造型还是纹饰，都独具风采，是东周时期最具代表性的楚文化铜鼎，它的主人就是春秋五霸之一的楚庄王的第五个儿子。与这组铜鼎一同出土的云纹铜禁是目前中国发现的最早使用失蜡法熔模工艺铸造的青铜器。1990 年在淅川徐家岭楚墓群出土的镶嵌绿松石神兽，高 48 厘米，体态矫健，动态神骏，龙首、虎身、龟足，作昂首、翘尾、四足后蹲状，头上兽角以 6 条蜿蜒盘绕的小龙构成，背部曲形架上站立一个同样动态的龙形奔兽。这件神兽通体装饰形态各异的龙凤纹饰，均以翠绿色的孔雀石镶嵌，龙首、舌、虎身、尾都是分别铸造，进而套合在一起，这件青铜神兽很可能是用来作为鼓架，如此造型设计独特、镶嵌考究的铜塑艺术品是极其罕见的，可称国之瑰宝。

4. Bronze Treasures of the Chu State in Henan

The Chu State was established in the early years of the Western Zhou Dynasty. Since the Spring and Autumn Period, Chu had moved northerly to the Central Plains. The vassal states in the Han-Huai valley were gradually attached to Chu and were eventually destroyed by it. Chu destroyed other states, and extended its land thousands of miles.It was the most powerful state in the south at that time, and showed its ambition to dominate the Central Pains. In the early years of the Warring States Period, Baiqi, the Qin general attacked Chu so that King Xiang of Chu retreated to Chencheng (now Huaiyang). Chu was finally destroyed by Qin.

Chu culture was popular in Hunan, Hubei, Henan and Anhui provinces. Henan was an important area for the origin and development of Chu culture. The people of Chu had written their glorious poems and articles in the Central Plains. According to statistics, there are more than 200 Chu tombs excavated in Henan, such as the bronze vessels unearthed in Changtaiguan of Xinyang, the Xia Temple of Xichuan, Chuwangcheng of Xinyang and Chen Chu cemetery in Huaiyang. Wangziwu Ding, Wangsungao patent chime, bronze with cloud patterns, and a turquoise-inlaid bronze beast in the Xia Temple of Xichuan are the best bronze objects among Chu (and even superior when compared with the best of Chinese bronze ware in general) showing superb casting technology.

Since 1970s, a number of cemeteries of the Chu nobles have been found in Xichuan County, Henan Province, especially the Chu tombs excavated at both the Xia Temple from 1978 to 1979 and Heshangling from 1990 to 1991, Xichuan County, which have attracted worldwide attention. Among the many bronze objects unearthed, the ritual instruments are the most eye-catching. These utensils are not only tall in shape, magnificent in ornamentation, but also exquisite in casting, and many of them have inscriptions. The bronze wares in Xichuan tomb with their smart and gorgeous modeling style, and their delicate patterns of flat-winged insects form the main ornamentation with a strong sense of rhythm that reflects the rich romantic imagination and vitality of the Chu people. In 1978, there were 7 pieces of Wangziwu Ding unearthed from the Chu tombs at the Xia Temple with the same shape and similar size. The whole set of bronze *ding* were majestic in shape, well-made,

淅川下寺楚墓群出土的王子午鼎

Bronze Wangziwu Ding, Unearthed from the Chu Tombs at Xiasi, Xichuan County

此外，由于在战国初年，楚顷襄王辗转流亡，继而退至陈城（今淮阳），在河南境内留下了大量足迹，信阳、淮阳、固始、新蔡、上蔡、正阳等地都发现有大型楚国贵族墓葬。如 2006 年在上蔡故城附近发现的 2 座大型楚国贵族墓葬，均为诸侯或王级的"甲"字形大墓，特别是采取了积沙积石和假棺的埋葬手段，有效防御了 2000 多年来的盗墓行为，使得墓中保存下大量精美的青铜器。在 40 余件带有铭文的青铜器上，出现了"楚王孙""陈公""曾侯""吴土""许公"等许多重要的历史人名和地名。

从西周晚期开始，楚国青铜器显露出楚文化特有的风采，到春秋早期，楚国青铜器已经摆脱周文化风格青铜器传统的束缚，新的楚式青铜器开始出现。楚国特有的束腰平底的升鼎、小口带盖的罐形康鼎、折沿束颈的繁鼎，其余如高足鬲、盆体敦、龙耳簋、浴缶、尊缶、鉴缶、盘尊、龙首提梁盉等，其精美程度都为北方诸侯国青铜器所不及。楚国青铜器繁缛夸张的装饰和纹饰，表现出一方先民独特的审美习俗，与楚国先进的青铜铸造工艺分不开。特别是失蜡法的出现，使得青铜器成为玲珑剔透的艺术品，人文的艺术风韵压倒了神秘的祭器用途。楚国青铜器铭文

richly decorated, and welded in accordance with the best standards of the day. This bronze *ding* was unique in shape and ornamentation, and was the most representative bronze *ding* of Chu culture in the Eastern Zhou Dynasty. Its owner was King Zhuang of Chu, one of the five tyrants in the Spring and Autumn Period. In 1990, the turquoise-inlaid mythical beast unearthed from Chu tombs in Xujialing, Xichuan, is 48cm high. The beast is vigorous with a dragon's head, tiger's body, and turtle's feet, holding its head high, cocking its tail and crouching behind its four legs. The horns on its head are made up of six winding little dragons, and a dragon-shaped galloping beast with the same dynamics stands on a curved frame on its back. This beast is decorated with different patterns of dragon and phoenix. The beast's dragon head, tongue, tiger body, and tail are all cast separately, and then set together. This bronze beast was likely to be used as a drum stand. The bronze in unique design is considered as the national treasure.

In addition, in the early Warring States Period, King Xiang of Chu exiled and then retreated to Chencheng (now Huaiyang). Large tombs of the Chu nobles were found in Changtaiguan in Xinyang, Pingliangtai in Huaiyang, Gushi, Xincai, Shangcai, and Zhengyang. For example, in 2006, two large tombs of the Chu nobles found near the old city of Shangcai were in form of the Chinese character "甲", in which the burial methods of accumulating sand, stones, and fake coffins were employed to effectively prevent grave-robbing for more than 2,000 years, so a large number of exquisite bronze wares could be preserved in the tombs. On more than 40 bronze objects with inscriptions, many important historical names and place names such as "Chuwangsun", "Chengong", "Zenghou", "Wutu" and "Xugong" can be found.

From the late Western Zhou Dynasty, Chu bronze ware showed the unique style of Chu culture. By the early Spring and Autumn Period, Chu bronze ware had got rid of the shackles of Zhou bronze tradition. Shengding, Kangding, Fanding and other bronze objects are all exquisite in the northern vassal states. The elaborate decoration and ornamentation of bronze ware in Chu showed the unique aesthetic custom, inseparable from the advanced bronze casting technology in Chu. In particular, the lost wax casting method made bronze wares exquisite, and its artistic charm overwhelmed the mysterious sacrificial vessels. The inscriptions on bronze wares in Chu are full of changes. The Chu were experts at

波折流丽，富于变化，楚人善于运用鸟虫书体的美术字，用特殊的楚国辞语、整齐有致的韵文，传达出楚人遣词造句和书写中唯美的思维习性。

淅川下寺楚墓群出土的王孙诰编钟
Bronze Wangsungao Chimes, Unearthed from the Chu Tombs at Xiasi, Xichuan County

淅川徐家岭楚墓群出土的镶嵌绿松石神兽
Bronze Beast Inlaid with Turquoise, Unearthed from the Chu Tombs at Xujialing, Xichuan County

5. 韩、赵、魏青铜器

公元前585年，晋景公迁都至新田，此后，晋国六卿势力渐强，相

employing the fine calligraphy of birds and insects. They used special Chu words and neat rhymes to convey their thought.

淅川下寺楚墓发掘现场
Excavation Site of the Chu Tombs at Xiasi, Xichuan County

淅川下寺楚墓群出土的云纹铜禁
Bronze Jin with Cloud Patterns, Unearthed from the Chu Tombs in Xiasi, Xichuan County

5. Bronze Treasures of the Han State, the Zhao State and the Wei State

In 585 BC, King Jing of the Jin Dynasty moved the capital to Xintian. Since

互倾轧，到公元前453年，韩、赵、魏灭知氏，三家分晋。公元前403年，周威烈王正式册命三家为诸侯，韩、赵、魏作为大夫夺权而后封侯的新兴国家，以其强盛的实力，进入战国七雄之列。随着列国的强盛和自身文化特点的形成，韩、赵、魏三国青铜器进入了空前繁荣时期，在继承西周以来晋国传统器型基础上，增加了方座豆、盖豆、敦、各类鸟兽形尊等崭新的青铜器类，将传统的青铜食器系列如鼎、簋、鬲、舟、盘，变为鼎、豆、壶、盘组合为主，与同时期的南方楚国、西方秦国的青铜器有明显的文化差异。以韩、赵、魏为中心的中原系列青铜器自此成为战国时期绚丽的风景。

韩国被封为诸侯国时，都城已几经迁移，韩景侯定都于阳翟故城（今河南禹州）。公元前375年，韩国灭郑，迁都于郑国都城（今新郑），直到公元前230年被秦国所灭。韩国境内出土大量贵族墓葬、窖藏器物，如洛阳金村韩墓、新郑白庙范村青铜兵器窖藏、新郑胡庄韩王陵区国君大墓等。1971年在郑韩故城东城东南部的白庙范村发现的青铜兵器窖藏坑，出土戈、矛、剑等青铜兵器180件，其中170余件上都带有铭文，少者1字，多者33字，多于铜戈的内部或矛的骹部，分铸款、刻款和先铸后刻三种记铭方式，年代约在公元前310—前231年的韩襄王和韩王安时期。这些兵器及铭文对于我们今天研究战国晚期韩国的历史地理、文字形态、冶铸官署设置、兵器形制及铸造工艺，具有非同一般的意义。

赵国是三国中地理位置最靠北的国家，北与燕、林胡、楼烦等国接壤，东与中山、齐毗邻，南临卫、魏、韩中原诸国。赵国最早建都于晋阳（今山西太原），公元前425年迁于中牟（今河南鹤壁市西），公元前386年又都邯郸（今河北邯郸）。公元前222年，赵国被秦国所灭。赵国一直处于胡汉交错地带，有关赵国考古发现大都集中在今山西、河南、河北三省，河南境内的赵国青铜器主要发现于北部的安阳林州等地。林州大菜园东周墓地近年来发现了700多座战国时期赵国墓葬，其中有不少贵族大墓和车马坑，出土了1200余件套的青铜礼乐器、车马和生活用具，

then, the six officials of the Jin State had gradually become stronger and combated with one another. By 453 BC, Han, Zhao and Wei had destroyed the Zhi family, and the three families divided the Jin State into three parts. In 403 BC, King Wei Lie of the Zhou Dynasty officially named Han, Zhao and Wei as Marquis. Since then the three as the emerging states seized power and joined the seven heroes of the Warring States with their strong strength. With the prosperity of the states and the formation of their own cultural characteristics, the bronze objects in Han, Zhao and Wei reached an unprecedented excellence. Inheriting the traditional shapes of the Jin State since the Western Zhou Dynasty, brand-new bronze wares were produced, and the traditional bronze food vessel combinations of *ding*, *gui*, *li*, *zhou* and *pan* were changed into new ones of *ding*, *dou*, *hu* and *pan*. Since then, the bronze wares of the Central Plains, especially in Han, Zhao and Wei, had become the dazzling scenery in the Warring States Period.

When the Han State was entitled a vassal state, its capital had been moved several times, and Jinghou of Han made his capital in the old city of Yangzhai (now Yuzhou, Henan). In 375 BC, Han destroyed Zheng and moved its capital to the capital of Zheng (now Xinzheng) until it was destroyed by the Qin in 230 BC. A large number of noble tombs and vessels had been unearthed in Han, such as the Han Tomb in Jincun Village, Luoyang, the bronze weapons hoarded in Baimiaofan Village, Xinzheng, and the great tomb of the king in Hanwang Tomb Park, Huzhuang Village, Xinzheng. In 1971, 180 bronze weapons, such as swords and spears, were unearthed from the bronze weapons storage pit in Baimiaofan Village, southeast of the old city of Zheng and Han. Among them, more than 170 pieces had inscriptions, ranging from one character to 33 characters, which were more than the inside of bronze weapons or the chin of spears. There were three inscription methods: casting, engraving, and first casting and then engraving. The age was about 310-231 BC. These weapons and inscriptions are of extraordinary significance for us to study the history, geography, characters, the establishment of smelting and casting authorities, the shape of weapons and the casting technology of Han in the late Warring States Period.

The Zhao State was bordering Yan, Linhu, Loufan, and other states in the north, Zhongshan and Qi in the east, and Wei（卫）, Wei（魏）and Han in the south. The capital of Zhao was first established in Jinyang (now Taiyuan, Shanxi Province),

有青铜鼎、敦、方彝、鉴、壶、盘等，还首次发现了赵国的青铜编钟，包括钮钟、甬钟和镈钟，还有与之相配套的石磬。与前期相比，赵国青铜器已经由厚重神秘变得轻巧灵动，整体造型优雅，精致独特，其纹饰采用多种镂刻、镶嵌、模印的工艺手法，追求一种细腻多变、复杂新颖的风格，充分显示了赵国青铜文化的高超水平。

魏国是三家分晋后最先强大起来的国家。魏国原都于安邑（今山西夏县西北），公元前361年东迁大梁（今河南开封）。大梁因处于黄河河道之特殊地理位置，文物遗迹埋藏较深，考古发掘成果甚微，只在传世铜器中有大梁司寇鼎存在。在今河南辉县的固围村、赵固村，汲县的山彪镇，豫西的三门峡等地发现了魏国贵族墓葬。山彪镇的发掘始于1928年，出土了大量精美文物，其中一号墓仅青铜器就有1447件，占此墓出土文物的90%以上，包括青铜列鼎、簠、鬲、甗、簋、豆、壶等器类。在历年来发现的魏国青铜器中，有不少集设计、工艺、实用为一体的杰出代表，如汲县山彪镇出土的鸟兽纹贯耳铜壶，线条流畅，造型优美，颈部以下通体铸鸟兽纹，体现了魏国青铜铸造技术的高超水平。还有山彪镇一号墓的水陆攻战纹青铜鉴，将红铜嵌于预先铸就的青铜器身凹槽内，以上、中、下三层图案表现战士与周边部族鏖战的场景，如徒卒对射、舟师交攻、长枪短兵、滚石檑木、云梯旌旗等古代两军对峙时的交战场面，涉及兵将多达286人，惨烈与恢宏构成了青铜艺术之绝顶风光。1975年三门峡上村岭战国墓地出土跽坐人铜灯，高48.9厘米，铜灯由跽坐人、灯架和灯盘三部分分铸铆接而成，可进行拆装，且各部分之间对接紧密，整体髹漆尽脱。跽坐人偏髻、束冠，身着右衽深衣，腰系以带钩扣合的革带，双手合擎"Y"形灯架，架上托环形灯盘，盘内设烛座三个。跽坐人面部结构准确，表情沉静，发丝清晰可辨，形体塑造规矩严谨，将举灯人谦卑、恭顺的形象表现得淋漓尽致。

魏国青铜器以其清新的风格、精巧的制作为人们所珍视，特别是利用动物之立体雕塑装饰器身的做法，圆壶上的华盖立鸟、贝纹鼎上的三

moved to Zhongmu (now west of Hebi, Henan Province) in 425 BC, and was in Handan (now Handan, Hebei Province) in 386 BC. In 222 BC, Zhao was destroyed by the Qin. Zhao had always been in the interconnecting areas between Hu and Han. The archaeological discoveries of Zhao had been concentrated in Shanxi, Henan and Hebei. Bronze wares of Zhao in Henan had been mainly found in Anyang which lies in the north of Henan. In recent years, more than 700 tombs of Zhao in the Warring States Period have been found in the Eastern Zhou cemetery of Dacaiyuan, Linzhou, including tombs of the noble and carriages. More than 1,200 sets of bronze ritual instruments, carriages, and household appliances including bronze *ding*, *dun*, *fangyi*, *jian*, pot and *pan*, have been unearthed. Bronze chimes and *qing* have also been found for the first time. Compared with the earlier period, the bronzeware of Zhao had become light and smart, with elegant and exquisite overall shape. It adopted a variety of carving, inlaying, and stamping techniques, and pursued a delicate, changeable, complex and novel style.

The Wei State was the first to become strong among the three states. The capital was located in Anyi (now northwest of Xia County, Shanxi), then moved to Daliang (now Kaifeng, Henan) in 361 BC. Due to the special geographical position of Daliang in the Yellow River, the cultural relics were deeply buried, and the archaeological excavation results were minimal. Only the Sikou Ding exists. Tombs of Wei nobles were found in Guwei Village, Zhaogu Village of Huixian County, Shanbiao Town of Jixian County, and Sanmenxia City. The excavation of Shanbiao Town began in 1928, and a large number of exquisite cultural relics were unearthed, among which M1 only had 1,447 bronze objects, accounting for more than 90% of the cultural relics found in this tomb, including a set of five bronze tripod heads, as well as *gui*, and pots. Wei bronze wares had been prized for its method of decorating the body with three-dimensional sculptures of animals, such as the canopy bird on the round pot, the crouching beast on the shell tripod, and the sacrificial beast carrying the lotus statue plate, all of which have inherited the bronze casting characteristics of the Jin State whose craftsman were adept at using animals patterns to decorate the body of bronzeware. The bronze objects of the Wei State reflect the superb bronze inlay technology. In particular, the bronze ware with the water and land battles from Tomb No.1 in Shanbiao Town embed

伏兽、背驮莲花尊盘的牺兽等，均继承了晋国善于利用动物来装饰青铜器身的青铜铸造特性，并有新的创造。

汲县山彪镇出土的鸟兽纹贯耳铜壶
Bronze Hu with Bird and Animal Patterns, Unearthed at Shanbiao, Jixian County

三门峡市上村岭出土的跽坐人铜灯
Bronze Lamp in the Shape of a Kneeling Man, Unearthed at Shangcunling, Sanmenxia City

red copper in the groove of the precast bronze body. The upper, middle and lower layers of patterns show the scenes between the soldiers and the surrounding tribes involving as many as 286 soldiers. In 1975 the bronze lamp with a figure sitting on heels is 48.9cm high, which was riveted after the figure, the lamp bracket and the support were separately cast. This lamp can be disassembled and then assembled, and its three parts are connected with one another. Its painting was removed naturally. The figure sat on his heels with the bun on one side, a hat on the top of his head, the featured garment of Han nation, the leather belt around the waist. He put the hands together holding a Y-shaped lamp bracket with a round plate on it. In this plate there are three candle posts. The figure has the exact organs in calmness, clean hair, fine shape which is the typical image of a candle-holding person with the humble attitude.

The bronze wares of Wei have been prized by people for their fresh styles and exquisite workmanship, especially, the method of using three-dimensional animal sculpture to decorate the body of the bronze object. Such as the canopy bird on the round pot, the crouching beast on the shell tripod, and the sacrificial beast carrying the lotus statue plate, all inherited the bronze casting characteristics of the Jin State which were good at using animals to decorate the body of the bronze ware, and furthermore made new creations.

三门峡市上村岭出土的羽纹铜扁壶

Bronze Hu with Feather Designs, Unearthed at Shangcunling, Sanmenxia City

6. 豫南汉淮地区诸小国青铜器

汉淮地区处于中原和荆楚之间，历来是上古民族交错杂居之地，既有复杂的历史渊源，又有错综的文化形态。西周初年周王在此地分封了许多同姓和异姓诸侯国，作为周王室的南土屏障。在东周时期长期的列国兼并争霸中，这些小国先后为强国吞并，极少能留下历史事迹，只有吴国、黄国、樊国、养国、许国、曾国等小诸侯国墓葬出土的风格各异的青铜器，述说着一代诸侯的繁华旧事。

1978 年，在固始侯古堆发现了一座"甲"字形大墓，随葬了 9 件鼎、1 套编镈、1 套编钟等大批青铜器，墓主人为勾敔（音同吴）夫人，也就是宋国国君宋景公（公元前 516—前 441 年）的妹妹、吴国太子夫差的夫人。宋景公将其妹季子远嫁吴国，并为她制作了大批的嫁妆，包括铜器、漆器和陶瓷器。但季子在 30 岁左右便去世了，其夫家将其嫁妆悉数由陪嫁品转为陪葬品而掩埋在墓冢内，用来显示她的特殊地位。

黄国作为淮河流域的小国，长期与楚国抗衡，后来在公元前 648 年被楚国所灭。黄国故城位于今河南潢川县西北。在今天的罗山、光山、潢川等地都出土了不少珍贵的黄国文物，时代多为春秋早期。1983 年，在黄国故城西南的光山县宝相寺发现春秋早期偏晚的"黄君孟"夫妇合葬墓。出土青铜器中有"黄君孟自作行器"和"黄子作黄夫人孟姬"之铭，其墓地有高大的封冢和庞大的椁室结构，并设置边箱分放器物。这种墓葬形式为后来多数楚国贵族所承袭。黄国青铜器蕴含着中原文化和楚文化融合的诸多因素，表明了黄国处于两大文化区域之间的独特地位。

蔡国是春秋时期中原诸侯国中最早臣服于楚国的，春秋晚期又依附于吴国，至公元前 447 年，最终被楚国所灭。因受楚国胁迫，蔡国曾三次迁都。今河南上蔡县城关一带发现的蔡国故城遗址，西周早期始建，春秋战国仍修筑使用。2006 年，在上蔡发现了一批春秋时期蔡国的中

三门峡市上村岭出土的错金银豹镇
Leopard-shaped Bronze Zhen Inlaid with Gold and Silver, Unearthed in Shangcunling, Sanmenxia City

6. Bronze Treasures in Hanhuai Region in Southern Henan

The Hanhuai region lies between the Central Plains and Jingchu (now Hubei Province). Ancient nationalities intermingled in the area and produced intricate cultures and a complicated history. In the early Western Zhou Dynasty, many vassal states had been granted the territories here, which served as the southern land barrier of the royal family. During the long-term annexation and hegemony of nations in the Eastern Zhou Dynasty, these small states were successively annexed by powerful ones, and few historical events about them were recorded. Only the bronze vessels of varying styles from the tombs of these small vassal states, such as Wu, Huang, Fan, Yang, Xu, and Zeng, bear witness to their former prosperity.

In 1978, a tomb in the form of the Chinese character "甲" was found where 9 *ding*, a set of plaiting *bo*, a set of chimes and other large number of bronze objects were found. The owner of the tomb was Mrs. Gou Wu, the sister of King Jing of the Song State. The king married his sister Jizi to the Wu State with a large number of dowries including bronze, lacquer ware, and ceramics. However, Jizi died young around the age of 30, and her husband's family buried all her dowries in her tomb to show her special status.

As a small state along the Huaihe River, the Huang State after a long fight with the Chu State was finally destroyed by Chu in 648 BC. The old city of

小型墓葬，出土了一批青铜礼器。

接受南北两大主流文化渗透的还有与黄国处于同样地位的樊国，有信阳南山嘴出土的樊君夔与夫人龙嬴青铜器；番国，有潢川彭店所出番君伯龙器、固始侯古堆大墓所出番子成周编钟；姬姓曾国，有新野出土的曾子伯青铜器群；昶国，有桐柏左庄出土的昶伯、昶仲器物；养国，有桐柏月河贵族大墓所出的青铜器。2002年，叶县发现了几座春秋时期许国贵族墓葬，所出土的青铜器更为明显地将中原与南方楚文化两种风格汇于一处。在这些小国器物中，春秋早期的沿用西周旧制，春秋中晚期的追随荆楚新风，正说明汉淮二水间是中原与楚争锋之所在。随着周王朝日渐没落，这些江淮间的诸侯小国从周王室之南国屏障而变为大国弱肉强食的对象。江淮小国出土的青铜器风格的演变，反映了这些国家为楚文化所同化的历史过程。

固始侯古堆出土的乳钉纹圆盒
Round Bronze Box with Boss Designs, Unearthed at Hougudui, Gushi County

Huang lies in the northwest of Huangchuan County, Henan Province. Many precious Huang cultural relics mostly in the early Spring and Autumn Period have been unearthed in Luoshan, Guangshan, Huangchuan. In 1983, the joint burial tomb of Huang Junmeng and his wife in the early Spring and Autumn Period, was found in Baoxiang Temple, Guangshan County, southwest of the old city of the Huang State. The unearthed bronze ware came with inscriptions and the cemetery has a tall burial place and a huge chamber structure with boxes set aside for storing objects. This kind of burial was inherited by most Chu nobles later. The bronze wares of Huang integrated the Central Plains culture and Chu culture, which indicates that the Huang State enjoyed a unique position between the two cultures.

The Cai State was the first vassal state in the Central Plains during the Spring and Autumn Period to submit to the Chu State. In the late Spring and Autumn Period, it was attached to the Wu State, and finally destroyed by Chu in 447 BC. Being coerced by Chu, Cai moved its capital three times. Today, the site of the old city of Cai was found in the Chengguan area of Shangcai County, Henan Province. It was built from the early Western Zhou Dynasty, and mended to use in both the Spring and Autumn Period and the Warring States Period. In 2006, a number of small and medium-sized tombs of Cai in the Spring and

固始侯古堆出土的蟠虺纹提梁盉

Handled Bronze He with Pan Hui Patterns, Unearthed at Hougudui, Gushi County

光山县黄君孟墓出土黄君孟鼎

Bronze Huangjunmeng Ding, unearthed from the Huangjunmeng tomb, Guangshan county

光山县黄君孟墓出土的黄夫人壶

Bronze Hu, Unearthed from the Huangjunmeng Tomb, Guangshan County

7. 河南东周青铜器的铸造技术和特点

东周时期是中国历史上重要的技术创新时代。表现在青铜器上，主要是铸造技术与艺术加工两个方面，显著的发展是大量使用了分铸法，并发明了失蜡法熔模铸造、线刻画像、模印、镶嵌纯铜和珠玉、错金银、

Autumn Period were discovered in Shangcai, and a number of bronze ritual vessels were unearthed.

The Fan State like the Huang State was influenced by the two cultures of the north and the south where today bronze objects used by the king of Fan and his wife were unearthed in Nanshanzui, Xinyang. In the Fan State bronze wares used by the king were unearthed in Pengdian Village, Huangchuan County and Fanzichengzhou chimes in Hougudui tomb in Gushi County. In the Zeng State (ruled by the Zeng family) a bronze group of zengzibo were excavated; similar findings were made in the former Chang and Yang states. In 2002, the tombs of the nobles of the Xu State were discovered in Yexian County. The unearthed bronze objects more obviously combined the Central Plains culture and the southern Chu culture. These utensils of other smaller states, which followed the old system of the Western Zhou Dynasty in the early Spring and Autumn Period as well as the new style of Jingchu in the middle and late Spring and Autumn Period, show that the Central Plains and Chu fought over the forts connecting the Han and Huai rivers . With the decline of the Zhou Dynasty, these small vassal states between the Yangtze and Huai rivers from the southern barrier of the royal family became the objects the big states fought over. The evolution of bronze vessels unearthed in these small states in the Yangtze and Huai rivers region reflects the assimilation process of these states by Chu culture.

7. The Casting Technology and Artistic Processing of Bronze Treasures During the Shang Dynasty and the Zhou Dynasty in Henan

The Eastern Zhou Dynasty was an important era of technological innovation in Chinese history, especially in casting technology and artistic processing of bronze vessels. Its remarkable development lies in the extensive use of split casting, and the invention of the lost wax investment casting, line portrait, back stamping, pure copper and pearl jade inlaying, gold and silver rubbing, gilding, welding and other new processes and technologies. Henan was the main battlefield for the powers in the Eastern Zhou Dynasty and also the main position of the birth and application of various advanced production technologies. Many advanced technologies and techniques of bronze casting were first discovered in Henan.

In the technology of bronze casting, the first improvement was the separating

鎏金、焊接等新工艺和新技术。河南地区是东周列国争雄的主战场，也是各类先进生产技术诞生和应用的主阵地，有不少青铜铸造的先进技术和工艺最早发现于此。

在青铜器铸造技术方面，一是分铸和焊接工艺的提高。在春秋以前，大型青铜器主要采用分铸法，将预先铸好的附件嵌入器身范内，在浇铸器身时将附件拼接而成。而在新郑、辉县等地发现的春秋时期青铜器中，往往是器身和附件单独做模，分别铸造，再将附件焊接在器身上。在新郑青铜器中就有不少能看到附耳、足、附加装饰物与器身之间的焊接现象。这种分铸焊接法，省工省时，效率高。分铸法的广泛应用，除了使产品趋于规范化外，还便于处理形制极为复杂的铸件，创造出气势雄伟、结构复杂的艺术作品，新郑出土的莲鹤方壶就是突出的例证。二是失蜡法的采用。失蜡法是一种全新的青铜铸造技术，春秋以前的青铜器都是用范铸法铸造，淅川下寺春秋晚期楚墓出土了中国最早的失蜡法铸造青铜器——云纹铜禁，其禁体、附兽等均为失蜡法铸造。失蜡法是一种精密铸造技术，也称熔模法。其方法是将石蜡精心雕琢成所需要的器型，也就是蜡模；再用调制过滤好的细泥浆逐次淋浇蜡模，并预留好多个浇口，使其成为泥质的模型；模型晾干后入窑烘烤，内部的蜡模融化后从浇口流出，从而形成型腔；趁热从浇口注入冶炼好的铜液，待铜液凝固后再清除模壳，这样就获得了精美的铸件。

在青铜器艺术加工方面，一是镶嵌纯铜工艺的出现。春秋时期开始在青铜器上镶嵌纯铜，然后将其磨平，显出光泽，从而形成精美的镶嵌图案。在卫辉山彪镇和辉县琉璃阁、固围村等地的战国墓中，出土有各类青铜器，其中有一些镶嵌着由金、银、玉石等多种质料构成的精美图案。二是春秋中晚期始见于南方青铜兵器上的错金银工艺，战国初期已经在河南地区推广，主要是在青铜礼器表面错嵌金银图案。20世纪20年代在洛阳金村被盗掘的东周王室大墓中的一批鼎、簋、壶、扁壶、镜等青铜器，就采用了错金银工艺，通体饰以各种云纹、龙纹等纹饰，极为精致。

of casting and welding. Before the Spring and Autumn Period, large bronze vessels were mainly cast separately into which the precast accessories were embedded and then the accessories were spliced through casting. However, among the bronze objects found in Xinzheng, Huixian and other places during the Spring and Autumn Period, their body and accessories were molded and cast separately and then the accessories were welded to the body. Among the bronze vessels excavated from Xinzheng, the ears, feet, and accessories were found to be welded to the body. This split casting welding method saved labor and time. The wide application of the split casting method not only makes the products more standardized, but also facilitates the processing of castings with complex shapes to create magnificent works of art with complex structures. The Lotus Crane Square Pot unearthed in Xinzheng was an exemplary discovery. The second improvement in bronze casting and welding was the adoption of the lost wax casting method. Before the Spring and Autumn Period bronze wares were all cast by the mold casting method. The earliest casting bronze in China was Bronze Jin with Cloud Patterns unearthed from a tomb of the Chu State in Xiasi, Xichuan County during the late Spring and Autumn Period. Its body and attached animal patterns were all cast by the lost wax casting method. This method is a kind of precision casting technology, also known as the investment method. The method is to carve paraffin wax into the required shape, that is, wax mold; Then, the wax mold is poured successively with fine mud that had been modulated and filtered, and a plurality of gates were reserved to make it a mud model; After the mold was dried, it was baked in a kiln, and the internal wax mold melted and flowed out of the gates, thus forming a cavity. The molten copper was injected from the gates while it was hot, and then the mold shell was removed after the molten copper solidified, thus producing a beautiful cast.

In the artistic expression of the bronze ware, the first aspect was the technology of inlaying pure copper. In the Spring and Autumn Period, bronze vessels were inlaid with pure copper, and then polished to show its luster, forming a beautiful mosaic pattern. (From the tombs of the Warring States Period in Shanbiao Town, Weihui County, and Liulige Village and Guwei Village in Huixian County, various bronze objects were unearthed, some of which were inlaid with exquisite patterns made of gold, silver, jade and other materials.) The

这种工艺技术是先在青铜器的铸范上预留纹饰凹槽，待器物铸成后，再在凹槽内镶嵌金、银、红铜、铅等金属丝条，然后敲打使其牢固，最后反复打磨出光泽。由于青铜的颜色较暗，而金、银等色彩鲜艳，从而形成富丽堂皇、婉转流畅的美丽花纹图案。此外，这时还出现了青铜刻镂图案工艺，在辉县赵固出土的青铜鉴上就有用细线刻镂的"大蒐礼"图案。

second aspect in the artistic expression of the bronze ware was the technology of rubbing gold and silver, which was first seen on bronze weapons of southern areas in the middle and late Spring and Autumn Period and was popularized throughout Henan during the early Warring States period. This was mainly accomplished by rubbing and embedding gold and silver patterns on the surface of bronze ritual vessels. In the 20th century, a batch of bronze objects such as *ding*, *gui*, pot, flat pot, mirror, etc., which were stolen and excavated in Jincun Village, Luoyang in the 1920s, made of gold and silver, were decorated with various moire and dragon patterns. The first step was to reserve a decorative groove on the casting pattern of the bronze ware; The second was to embed gold, silver, red copper, lead and other metal wires into the groove after casting; The third was to beat it into place; And the fourth, to polish it to produce a luster. Moreover, the gold and silver pattern contrasts brilliantly against the dark bronze. Around this time, the process of carving bronze patterns also appeared, and the bronze inscription unearthed from Zhao Gu's tomb in Huixian County was engraved with the words "The Great Parade Rite" by using a fine thread.

四、河南商周青铜器在世界文明史上的地位

青铜器是中国古代文明的杰出代表。商周时期是中国青铜时代的核心阶段,也是中国青铜文明发展的高峰。商周青铜器以丰富奇特的造型、神秘缛丽的纹饰、精湛先进的铸造技术、典雅纪实的铭文而闻名于世,集中反映了中华文明形成与发展阶段的生产科技、艺术水平和历史源流,是中华文明的缩影与再现,也是中华民族对人类文明的巨大贡献。尤其是商周青铜器所承载的历史信息和文化基因,是玉器、瓷器、丝绸等其他中国特色文化载体都难以比拟和替代的。尽管中国不是唯一使用青铜器的地区,但是就青铜器的使用规模、铸造工艺、造型艺术及品种而言,世界上没有一个地方的青铜器能与中国商周青铜器相比拟。中国出土的商周青铜器的数量,远大于世界其他地区出土青铜器数量的总和,中国商周青铜器的种类,超出了世界其他地区青铜器种类的总和。这也是中国商周青铜器在世界文明史上占有独特地位并引起普遍关注的重要原因。

河南是华夏文明和中华民族的重要发祥地。一部河南史,半部中国史,自夏代至宋代的3000多年间,河南一直是中国政治、经济和文化的中心,几度形成人类文明的巅峰与辉煌。尤其是商周时期的河南,一直是商周王朝统治的核心地区,郑州、洛阳、安阳三座王都和犹如繁星密布的诸侯国,是商周时期青铜器铸造和技术革新的主要地区,率先诞生了青铜礼器和较大型的青铜兵器,奠定了中国青铜器以礼器为核心的发展基础,同时也开启了商周礼乐文明的灿烂篇章,甚至可以说,中国古代的礼乐文明就是诞生于河南,发展于河南,鼎盛于河南。河南商周青铜器分布范围广、数量大、种类多、时代全,而且大多数是考古发掘品,历史、艺术、科学价值极高,是其他地区所

IV. The Position of Henan's Shang and Zhou Bronze Ware in the History of World Civilization

Bronze wares are outstanding representatives of ancient Chinese civilization. Both the Shang Dynasty and the Zhou Dynasty are the core stages of the Chinese Bronze Age and the peaks of Chinese bronze civilization. Bronze wares are world-famous for their rich and peculiar shapes, mysterious ornamentation, exquisite and advanced casting technology, and elegant and documentary inscriptions, which reflect the production technology, artistic level and historical origin of the formation and development stage of Chinese civilization. They are the epitome and reappearance of Chinese civilization and the great contribution of the Chinese nation to human civilization. Especially the historical information and cultural genes carried by Shang and Zhou bronze wares are irreplaceable by other cultural carriers with Chinese characteristics such as jade, porcelain and silk. Although China is not the only area where bronze wares are used, there is no place in the world where bronze wares can be compared with those of Shang and Zhou in terms of scale of use, casting technology, plastic arts and varieties. Shang and Zhou bronze wares unearthed in China exceed the total sum of those in other parts of the world in both number and variety. This is the main reason why Shang and Zhou bronze wares occupy a unique position in the history of world civilization and attracted widespread concern in the world.

Henan is the birthplace of Chinese civilization and the Chinese nation. The history of Henan accounts for half of the history of China. From the Xia Dynasty to the Song, Henan had been the political, economic, and cultural center of China for more than 3,000 years, forming a peak in human civilization. Zhengzhou, Luoyang, and Anyang, as the ancient capitals in succession, were the main areas of bronze casting and technological innovation at that time. They took the lead in giving birth to bronze ritual vessels and larger bronze weapons, which laid the foundation for the development of Chinese bronze ware with ritual vessels at the forefront. The bronze objects at that time were widely distributed, large in quantity, various in variety. Most of them are archaeological excavations, which have extremely high historical, artistic, and scientific values. They are incomparable

难以比拟的，代表了中国商周青铜文明的最高水平，奠定了中华文明在世界文明史上的重要地位。

第一，河南商周青铜器数量大，种类多。截至目前，河南出土的商周青铜器已达数十万件，种类也极其丰富，不仅有酒器、水器、食器、兵器、礼器，还有车马器、农具、工具及各类生活用具等。

第二，河南商周青铜器分布地区广，且质量上乘。河南各地都发现有商周青铜器，这些青铜器风格各异，呈现出和而不同的艺术特色，其中有不少国之重器，如后母戊方鼎、"妇好"青铜鸮尊、莲鹤方壶等，制作精湛，具有撼人心魄的艺术感染力和视觉冲击力，几乎将人们带回那个遥远、神秘、充满宗教气息的时代。装饰艺术方面，纹饰繁缛华丽，铸造精细，并以各种动物纹和夸张、变异了的动物头部形象作为装饰，集中体现了中国古代青铜铸造的辉煌成就。河南商周时期的青铜器铸造已经能够根据不同的用途，准确把握合金比例用来控制硬度，这是当时世界其他地区所不具备的技术。

第三，河南商周青铜器铭文多。世界各地青铜器绝大多数没有铭文，只有印度等地的少量青铜器铸有很短的铭文。在中国1万多件带有铭文的商周青铜器中，河南出土的占据了很大比例，且时代连贯，还不乏鸿篇巨制。中国上古的文献资料非常稀缺，这些商周青铜器铭文记载了许多真实的历史，是研究中国古代历史不可替代的材料。

第四，以礼制容器为主的河南商周青铜器在世界青铜文化中独树一帜。在世界范围内，从印度河流域到巴尔干半岛，从米诺斯文明到迈锡尼文明，青铜器大多为武器、工具和装饰品，而以河南为代表的中国商周青铜器却以铸造难度较大、纹饰复杂的容器为主。这些青铜容器大多被赋予了礼制色彩，成为标识身份、等级地位甚至王朝政权的象征，如"九鼎八簋""钟鸣鼎食""定鼎中原"等礼制规范或历

to other parts of China, and represented the highest level of bronze civilization of Shang and Zhou, which have laid an important position of Chinese civilization in the history of world civilization.

First, the bronze wares of the Shang and Zhou dynasties in Henan were numerous and of various types. Up until now, hundreds of thousands of bronze objects unearthed in Henan are extremely rich in type, including not only wine vessels, water vessels, food vessels, weapons and ritual vessels, but also accessories to carriage, farm implements, tools, and household appliances.

Second, the Shang and Zhou Dynasty bronze wares were widely distributed and of high quality. Shang and Zhou bronze treasures have been found all over Henan. These bronze vessels have different styles, showing harmonious but different artistic features. Among them, there are many important instruments of the state, such as Houmuwu Rectangle Ding, Fu Hao Owl-shaped Zun, Lianhe Square Pot, etc., which are exquisitely made with breathtaking artistic appeal and visual impact, bringing the observer's imagination to that distant, mysterious, and religious era. They showed decorative arts with ornamentation, fine casting, animal patterns, exaggerated and varied animal head images, which embodies the brilliant achievements of ancient Chinese bronze casting. The bronze casting had accurately grasped the alloy proportion to control the hardness according to different uses, which was unavailable in other parts of the world at that time.

Third, bronze objects had long inscriptions during the Shang and Zhou dynasties. Most of them around the world had no inscriptions, only some in India had short inscriptions. Among more than 10,000 Shang and Zhou bronze wares with inscriptions in China, those in Henan alone account for a large proportion, and lasted through those years. As ancient Chinese literature is very scarce, these bronze inscriptions recorded history and are primary source material irreplaceable for the study of ancient Chinese history.

Fourth, the ritual vessels of the Shang and Zhou epoch are unique in the world bronze culture. In other regions of the world, from the Indus Valley to the Balkans, from Minoan to Mycenae civilization, bronze wares were mostly in the form of weapons, tools, and decorations, while the bronze wares of Shang and Zhou China, especially in Henan, were of cutting-edge casting technology and of complex ornamentation. Most of these bronze objects were endowed with the

史典故，都与青铜器有着直接联系，在国家最为重要的祭祀礼仪中发挥着不可替代的特殊功能。这些蕴含了丰富内涵和功能的青铜器在中国礼仪之邦形成初期，发挥了极为重要的作用，也是世界其他文明中所没有的。

function of ritual symbolizing the identity and social rank of their masters. For example, bronze wares in ritual norms or historical allusions such as the "Jiu Ding Ba Gui" system played a special function irreplaceable by any other material in the most important national sacrificial rites. These bronze objects played a very important role in the early development of Chinese rituals.

第三章

百花齐放——秦汉帝国时代河南青铜艺术的转型之路

Chapter 3

The Blossoming of Henan's Bronze Art Under the Qin and Han Empires

一、秦统汉继：传统礼器的延续

公元前221年，秦王嬴政灭六国，废除分封制，推行郡县制，统一文字、度量衡等，然而短短15年后，便被西汉取而代之。国家的政治、经济虽然实现了统一，但民众思想意识的同心却不是一朝一夕就能实现的。中原地区的河南是当时国家的核心区域，同时还是咸阳、长安的东方屏障。在今天河南的地域内，秦至汉初的文化遗存显现出不同的文化因素，主要还是延续了战国时期秦、三晋、楚及宗周等的文化影响。各个地域出土的青铜器均有较为明显的特点，传统的礼器仍在延续使用。

1. 秦汉时期传统礼器

从秦灭六国到西汉亡秦再现一统，这个时间是比较短暂的。各诸侯国的豪门贵族依然存在，从思想上来说，他们仍然会固守烙在内心深处的礼仪习俗，有相当一部分是世代传承的。故而，传统青铜礼器的流转在秦汉时期是一种长期存在的文化现象。国家形态虽然发生了变化，但是部分礼仪及其用器被传承下来，仍承载着此前的内涵。这类器物主要有鼎、圆壶、蒜头壶、提链壶、鈁、盒、匜等青铜器。泌阳县花园乡大曹庄和官庄村发现的秦人墓，均出土有典型秦文化因素的蒜头壶，这说明随着秦统一六国的步伐，大量的秦人因为战争、移民等情况留在了当地，但传承延续的仍然是秦文化的因素。三门峡陕县火电厂出土的圆壶、铜鼎、蒜头壶、铜鈁等，也有秦人移民的地域性特点。这些地方的汉代墓葬中出土的鼎、壶、鈁等青铜器与战国晚期至秦汉初期的造型没有明显区别，就是传统青铜礼器及其文化因素的长期延续。

I. Inheritance and Continuity: Qin Unification and Traditional Ritual Vessels

At the end of the Warring States Period, there were six states in China. One of them, the Qin, set about the destruction of the others. The work was complete by 221 BC, when Ying Zheng became the first emperor of the Qin Dynasty and reigned as Qin Shi Huang (r. 221-210 BC). But after 15 years Qin was destroyed and replaced by the Western Han Dynasty. At that time although Qin strengthened the central authority in politics and economics, it was hard to make all the citizens have the same mind. Henan in the Central Plains remained the core area of the country and also the eastern barrier of Xianyang and Chang'an. In today's Henan Province, cultural artifacts from the Qin and early Han dynasties reflect different cultural factors, primarily the cultural influences of the Qin, Sanjin, Chu and the Zhou territories of the Warring States Period. Bronze vessels unearthed in various areas show these characteristics and traditional ritual vessels were still in use.

1. Traditional Ritual Vessels During the Qin and Han Dynasties

Although the period from the Qin Dynasty uniting all states to the Western Han Dynasty destroying Qin is not long, the rich families of the vassal states still perpetuated the art motifs and forms of the Warring States era. In their thought they still remained the old rituals and traditions, so some of the rituals and traditions were inherited. By this way, the circulation of bronze utensils bear out this continuity. Although the dynasty was changed, some ritual and traditional vessels were kept. The excavated examples include the *ding*, round pot, garlic pot, pot with handles, *fang*, *he*, and *yi*. Garlic pots with typical Qin cultural factors were unearthed from Qin tombs in Dacaozhuang, and Guanzhuang, in Huayuan Township of Biyang County. The round pot, bronze ding, garlic pot, and fang unearthed from the Sanmenxia Thermal Power Plant also show the regional characteristics of Qin immigrants. There is no apparent difference between the shapes of the bronze vessels unearthed from the tombs of Han in these places from those of the late Warring States period, which suggests the inheritance of

蒜头壶
Garlic-Shaped Bronze Hu

2. 秦汉时期传统礼器的纹饰、工艺

青铜器的纹饰和器物功能存在着千丝万缕的联系，同时也是当时人们文化思想和审美观念的体现。秦汉时期传统青铜礼器是对战国时期一部分青铜器的延续，造型上是一脉相承的，部分器表纹饰也延续了下来。虽然人们的思想较之前有所变化，但对祖先留下来的文化仍旧恋恋不舍，只是原来器表纹饰代表的某种文化内涵，这时候不再具有了，纹饰更多可能仅表现装饰效果，反映出战国末期各诸侯国豪门贵族的遗老遗少们对过往的怀念。战国末期部分铸造工匠对于青铜铸造技艺的传承发挥了重要作用，他们将牢记在心里、熟练在手上的纹饰图案和工艺技能继续展现在青铜器上。因此，秦汉时期的传统青铜器上使用的纹饰、采用的工艺，依然是对战国时期的延续。受战国纹饰题材的影响较大，青铜器表面的几何线条纹饰、仿生的动物纹饰或动物的某个部位、幻化的龙凤形象、写实的植物形态等，与战国时期的纹样比较近似，但已有明显的

traditional bronze ritual vessels and their culture.

2. The Ornamentation and Craftsmanship of Traditional Ritual Vessels of the Qin and Han Dynasties

There is an inextricable link between the decoration and function of ancient Chinese bronze wares. The traditional bronze ceremonial vessels of the Qin and Han periods were a continuation of the bronze vessels of the Warring States Period, and the shapes were in line with each other. At the end of the Warring States Period, some of the foundry craftsmen played an important role in the transmission of bronze casting techniques, and they continued to display the ornamental patterns and craft skills that they had memorized and mastered. Thus, the ornamentation used and the craftsmanship employed on traditional bronze vessels of the Qin and Han periods remained a continuation of the Warring States Period. Strongly influenced by Warring States motifs, the geometric line decoration on the surface of the bronze, the imitation of animal motifs or a part of an animal, illusionary dragon and phoenix figures, and realistic plant forms were relatively similar to those of the Warring States Period, but there had been a clear trend toward dilution and many former motifs were no longer used.

变形云雷纹铜壶
Bronze Pot with Cloud and Thunder Patterns

淡化趋势，很多题材的纹饰这时候已经不再使用了。

传统青铜器的铸造工艺、铸造方法，主要还是传承延续东周时期的镶嵌、错金、错金银、錾刻、模铸和漆绘等。镶嵌和错金银工艺与之前相比没有明显的进步。錾刻工艺转移到新型铜器的纹饰塑造和文字的成形上。模铸技术有一些新变化，原本铜器上使用垫片是为了解决以前陶范设计上的缺陷而不得已采取的一种手段，秦汉时期的陶范套合技术完全可以避免使用垫片，但是在传统青铜礼器表面却密集而有规律地出现了垫片现象。这种情况不能说明模铸技术倒退了，而更可能是将垫片呈现色彩和器表色泽之间的色差现象通过有规律的布局，从而达到类似纹饰的一种效果。

几何纹及镶嵌工艺铜钫
Inlaid Bronze Fang with Geometric Patterns

3. 秦汉时期传统礼器铭文

铭文是商周青铜礼器的重要组成部分，其主要功能是记录王公贵族重要事件，包含歌功颂德、护佑子孙等内容，涉及政治、经济、礼仪、生活、文化等方方面面，是研究古代社会状况的重要信息载体。由于受工具条件的限制，商周青铜器铭文多为铸造的文字。到了春秋战国时期，

Traditional bronze casting techniques and casting methods were still mainly inherited from the Eastern Zhou period, such as inlay, inlay with gold, inlay with gold and silver, burin engraving, mold casting, and lacquer painting.

The inlaid and gold-inlaid and silver-inlaid processes had not improved significantly over those of previous eras. The burin process shifted to the shaping of ornamentation and text on the new bronze vessels. There were some new changes in mold-casting techniques. Originally, the use of shims on bronze vessels was a means of last resort to address the flaws in the design of the previous pottery workshop, and the pottery workshop overlay techniques of the Qin and Han periods completely avoided the use of shims, but the phenomenon of shims appeared densely and regularly on the surface of traditional bronze ritual objects. This did not indicate a regression in mold casting technology but was more likely to result from the difference between the color of the shims and the color of the surface of the vessel.

表面有密集垫片的铜钫
Bronze Fang with Shims on the Surface

3. Traditional Ritual Inscriptions of the Qin and Han Periods

Inscriptions were an important part of Shang and Zhou bronze ceremonial vessels, and their main function was to record important events of the princes

随着比铜更硬的刻画工具的出现，铭文除了铸造以外，新添了凿刻方法。铸造和凿刻这两种文字形成方式的不同，直接影响到铭文的呈现方式。铸造的文字多在器物的内腔空间呈现，在制作陶范和泥芯的时候就可以完成文字布局，注入铜液形成铜器时，铜器的文字也就一并形成了。铸造方式使文字形成的难度转移到了陶范制作上，相对而言是比较容易的。凿刻文字是在青铜器完成造型后才开始的一种凿刻行为，在凿刻过程中，需要有容纳凿刻工具及受力的空间，因此凿刻文字多呈现在器物的外表面。由于这种文字形成方式不受器物形成时间的约束，任何时间都可以在已经成型的器物上凿刻文字，故而从凿刻工具开始出现以后，凿刻文字就慢慢成为青铜器文字形成的主流。

秦汉时期，传统礼器上的文字延续了战国时期文字外露于表的趋势，多将铭文刻于器表，铭文内容一般包括所有者、容量、重量、制作者、时间等。从传统礼器凿刻文字来看，均有工官制作的记录，究其原因可能是该类器物主要是供应官员和王室等有较高身份的人使用，由中央或

表面凿刻文字涉及容量、重量、制作者、时间等内容且文字有多次凿刻现象
Multiple-Chiseled Characters on the Surface, Recording the Capacity, Weight, Maker, Time, etc.

and nobles, including songs of praise and virtue, protection of children and grandchildren, involving all aspects of politics, economy, etiquette, life, and culture. They are important information carriers for the study of ancient social conditions. Due to the limitations of tools, the Shang and Zhou bronze inscriptions were mostly cast texts. In the Spring and Autumn and Warring States periods, with the emergence of engraving tools harder than copper, inscriptions were not only cast, but also chiseled. The difference between the two types of text formation, namely casting and chiseling, directly affected the way inscriptions were presented. Cast text was mostly presented in the inner cavity space of the object and the layout of the text could be completed when the pottery model and clay core were made and when the copper liquid was injected to form the bronze, the text of the bronze was formed simultaneously. The casting method made it relatively easy to transfer the difficulty of text formation to the making of the pottery model. Chiseled writing was an act of chiseling that began only after the bronze finished being shaped. In the chiseling process, space was needed to accommodate the chiseling tool and the force, so chiseled writing was mostly presented on the outer surface of the object. Chiseled writing has ever become the mainstream ever since its use because the inscriptions can be added any time before or after the casting of the bronze vessels.

During the Qin and Han dynasties, the texts on traditional ceremonial vessels continued the trend of the Warring States Period of having texts leaked out onto the surface, with inscriptions mostly engraved on the surface of the vessels, which generally included the owner, capacity, weight, maker, and time. From the chiseled texts of traditional ceremonial vessels, there are records of their production by public officials, which may be explained by the fact that such vessels were mainly used by officials and people of high status such as the royal family, and were produced by central or local officials. This further indicates that the connotations carried by traditional ceremonial vessels did not disappear completely. The existence of multiple inscriptions on some of the wares is closely related to the way in which the texts were formed and where they were presented; the maker may have completed the basic form of the wares without inscribing the texts, but other users may also add the inscriptions on the surface of the bronze, resulting in the multiple chiseling on a single object.

地方工官直接生产。这也进一步说明传统礼器承载的内涵并未完全消失。在一部分器物上有多次凿刻文字的现象，这与文字的形成方式以及呈现位置有着密切的关系，制造者可能只是完成了器物的基本形态，并没有凿刻文字，器物在流转的使用者手中实现了文字的凿刻。不同使用者在器表凿刻文字，就会出现一件器物多次凿刻文字的现象。

除了铸造文字和凿刻文字，秦汉青铜礼器上还有彩绘文字。通常采用毛笔一类的绘制工具，将文字写在器物的表面，由于这类文字不能长久保存，所以使用这种方式的青铜器并不是很多。秦汉青铜器文字和战国青铜器文字有着明显的区别。战国时期，各个诸侯国都有自己的流行文字，同样一个字，在不同的国家书写形态也不同。秦国统一六国后，实现了文字统一，改大篆为小篆，全国通用。汉代以后，隶书开始流行，书写和辨识度更加有效。因此青铜礼器上的文字，秦代以小篆居多，汉代主要是隶书字体。这是国家意志对现实生活产生影响最直接的一种反映。

In addition to cast and chiseled texts, the Qin and Han bronze ritual objects also had painted texts. Usually a drawing tool such as a brush was used to write the text on the surface of the object, and not many bronze vessels used this method because this type of writing could not be preserved for long. There is a clear difference between Qin and Han bronze writing and Warring States bronze writing. During the Warring States Period, each vassal state had its own popular script, and the same character was written in different forms in different countries. After the Qin Dynasty unified the six states, the script was unified and changed from the big seal script to the small seal script, which was commonly used throughout the country. After the Han Dynasty, the clerical script became more popular and legible. Therefore, the writing on bronze ceremonial vessels was mostly in the small seal script of the Qin Dynasty, and mainly in clerical script during the Han Dynasty. This is one of the most direct reflections of the state's will having an impact on social life.

铜钫表面墨书文字

Ink-written Characters on the Surface of Bronze Fang

二、开拓创新：实用青铜器的繁荣

青铜器在中国开始出现时是实用工具，由西向东传到中原腹地后，才逐步附加了更多的内涵，并上升至礼仪用器的层面，且牢牢把握在贵族手中。东周以后，王室衰微，列强豪横，原有的礼制体系渐渐被打破，青铜器从礼制的高度开始下行，生活用器、日常用器渐渐增多。至秦汉时，青铜礼器的地位日渐式微，更倾向于实用。秦末农民起义一句"王侯将相宁有种乎"便是百姓想打破传统世俗的有力信号。汉立国后分封同姓、异姓诸侯于各地，使诸侯拥有大量的赋税收入，财富的集中和相对独立的管理权限给青铜器的多样化、实用化发展提供了条件。

1. 实用青铜器

青铜器在中国的出现，是从实用青铜器开始的。随着礼仪属性地位的逐步提高，原先实用的功能就渐渐淡化了。虽然商周时期铸造的绝大多数青铜器有着强烈的礼仪属性，但是整个青铜器时代，实用青铜器是一直存在的，只是我们在谈论青铜器的时候经常会将其划入一个相对独立的门类里，比如青铜兵器等。青铜兵器中的钺同样有着十分重要的礼仪性质，它是持有者拥有军权等的一种象征。春秋战国时期，诸侯纷争，变革潮流汹涌，学术流派众多，原来稳固健全的礼仪制度开始动摇，尊神敬鬼的意识形态开始向人本主义倾斜，思想上的变化导致青铜器发展更注重实用。这时期出现了更多为现实生活服务的器物，我们将其称为传统的实用青铜器，比如生活中常用的带钩、熏炉、灯、铜镜、铜镇等，虽然其中有些器物的装饰非常精美，运用了各种当时的工艺，但纹饰的精美并不能掩盖其实用功能。用青铜铸造便溺器的例子，也说明了青铜器在当时人心目中的高贵地位开始消失，更多注重的是它的实用功能。秦汉以后，这些器物多数仍在沿用，造型较战国时期略有变化。绝大多

II. Pioneering Innovation: The Prosperity of Practical Bronze Treasures

After bronze began to appear in China as a practical tool, it gradually took on more connotations and rose to the level of a ceremonial tool, firmly in the hands of the nobility, after it spread from the west to the Central Plains hinterland. After the Eastern Zhou Dynasty, with the decline of the royal family, the original ritual system was gradually broken, and bronze wares began to go down from the height of the ritual system, and the number of household and everyday wares gradually increased. In the Qin and Han dynasties, the status of bronze ceremonial wares gradually declined and became more popular and practical. The peasant uprising at the end of the Qin Dynasty was a powerful signal of the people's desire to break away from the traditional world. The concentration of wealth and relatively independent management authority provided the conditions for the diversification and practical development of bronze wares.

1. Practical Bronze Treasures

The emergence of bronze in China began with practical bronze vessels. As the status of ceremonial attributes gradually increased, the original practical function gradually faded away. Although most of the bronze wares cast during the Shang and Zhou periods had strong ceremonial properties, practical bronze vessels existed throughout the Bronze Age, but we often classify them into a relatively separate category such as bronze weapons. The battle-axe *yue* among the bronze weapons also had a very important ceremonial nature—it was a symbol that the holder had military power. During the Spring and Autumn and Warring States periods, when the states were in strife, the tide of change was raging, and there were many academic schools, the original solid and sound ceremonial system began to shake and the ideology of respecting the heavenly gods and ghosts began to tilt towards humanism. The change in thinking led to the development of bronze weapons that focused more on practicality. This period saw the emergence of more objects that served daily life such as belt hooks, smokers, lamps, bronze mirrors, and bronze weights that were commonly used in life. Although some of

数开始只注重实用性,如灯、带钩等,多素面,没有复杂的装饰。

卧虎形铜镇
Bronze Zhen Weights in the Shape of a Crouching Tiger

新兴实用青铜器类出现并流行于有汉一代,是汉代特有的青铜器类,通常用来满足人们日常生活的需要,多为饮食起居用具,基本没有礼仪属性。这一类器物的出现是汉代人们思想观念在青铜器上的反映,主要的种类有釜、甗、耳杯、碗、钵、卮、鐎斗、樽、盆、洗、染炉等数十种。

2. 实用青铜器的纹饰及工艺

汉代实用青铜器的纹饰受战国青铜器纹饰题材影响较小,也不受礼器属性的束缚,纹饰题材花样繁多。汉代继承了战国时期部分纹饰题材,如几何纹、花叶纹、云纹、动物纹等,同时又有所发展创新,龙纹、凤纹、云纹更加生动,花叶纹、动物纹趋向写实。汉代青铜器的铸造和装饰工艺大部分是对战国时期的继承,器物铸造多为范铸法,失蜡法的使用更为广泛。一次性将纹饰和器型铸成的青铜器数量明显减少,纹饰的形成更多采用后期加工的方式。比较典型的有樽、博山炉等器类,器身一般由传统的范铸法铸成,而盖为失蜡法铸成,通常先铸出盖重峦叠嶂的形态,再在器表刻出神仙人物、动物、植物和云气等,一件器物上集合了多种铸造方法和工艺。一些镂空结构的器物及小巧玩具多采用失蜡

青铜虎子，便溺用器
Tiger-shaped Bronze Huzi Urinal

these objects were very beautifully decorated, using various crafts of the time, the beauty of the decorations did not obscure their practical function. The example of a bronze casting for a commode also shows that the noble status of bronze in the minds of the people of the time began to disappear and more attention was paid to its practical function. After the Qin and Han dynasties, most of these wares were still in use, with slight changes in shape from the Warring States Period. The vast majority began to focus only on utility such as lamps and belt hooks, with mostly plain surfaces and no complex decoration.

Practical bronze wares emerged and became popular under the Han Dynasty. Eating and living utensils were common. The emergence of this class of wares was a reflection of the ideology of the Han Dynasty, and the main types include *fu*, *zeng*, ear cups, bowl, *bo*, *zhi*, *jiao dou*, *zun*, basins, *xi*, stoves, and dozens of others.

2. The Ornamentation and Craftsmanship of Practical Bronze Treasures

The ornamentation of practical bronze vessels in the Han Dynasty was diverse and less influenced by the ornamental themes of Warring States bronzeware. The Han Dynasty inherited some of the decorative motifs from the Warring States Period, such as geometric, leaf, cloud, and animal patterns. Yet, they expanded on them with dragon, phoenix, and cloud patterns becoming

法铸造。线刻工艺在汉代广泛使用,是对战国时期这类青铜工艺的延续和发展,是当时社会生活在青铜器纹饰上的审美选择。

失蜡法铸造的鎏金小动物
Gilt Bronze Animals Cast by the Lost Wax Casting Method

more vivid, and foliage and animal patterns more realistic. Most of the casting and decorative techniques of Han Dynasty bronze vessels were inherited from the Warring States Period and most of the objects were cast by the mold casting method and the lost wax casting method. The number of bronze objects with simultaneous casting of ornaments and shapes was reduced and the practice of casting ornaments separately became more typical. The body of the vessel was generally cast by the traditional van casting method, while the cover was cast by the lost wax method. This involved casting the form of the cover first, and then carving out the gods and goddesses, animals, plants and clouds on the surface of the vessel, yielding a collection of multiple casting methods and techniques on the same object. Some hollow structure objects and small toys were mostly cast by the lost wax casting method. The line engraving process was widely used in the Han Dynasty, a continuation and development of this type of bronze craft from the Warring States Period, and was an aesthetic choice for the social life of the time in the decoration of bronze objects.

What needs to be emphasized is the level of bronze casting in the Qin and Han periods. While Shang and Zhou bronze wares were characterized by thick and heavy shapes, complex ornamentation, and thick bodies, the Qin and Han bronze wares were very light and thin. From a technical point of view, as long as the raw materials were sufficient, the mold casting method was easier to operate but the mold was heavier and the cavity rather large. On the contrary, the thinner the object, the more difficult to cast. The casting of the bronze ware may result in failure so long as the outer mold and the inner core are not precisely matched. Han Dynasty artifacts as a whole were lighter and thinner, fully indicating that this stage of bronze model casting technology was an improvement. In addition, the Qin and Han bronze wares were much simpler to cast the form first and then to engrave the decoration on the surface of the object than to create the decoration on the pottery model first and then to shape and decorate the object at the same time when casting it.

This was an improvement in production tools that made it easier to produce and also shortened the production cycle and saved costs. For many relatively complex objects, the parts were mostly cast separately and then the whole object was assembled using mortise and tenon construction and overlay methods. This

需要强调的是秦汉时期的青铜铸造水平。商周青铜器以厚重为特点,造型复杂,纹饰繁缛,器身浑厚,而秦汉青铜器却十分轻薄。从技术的角度来说,只要原材料充足,使用范铸法铸造器物,厚重的器物范和芯的空腔就会大,操作起来比较容易。反而器物越薄,铸造难度越大,外范和内芯的套合只要有稍微的偏差,铸造出的器物可能就是残破的。汉代器物整体比较轻薄,充分说明这一阶段的青铜范铸技术较之前是有进步的。另外,相比于先在陶范上制作出纹饰,接着在铸造器物时实现造型和纹饰一并成形的工艺,秦汉青铜器采用先铸造器型,然后在器物表面刻画纹饰的方法就要简单多了。这是生产工具进步带来的制作上的方便,同时也缩短了制作周期,节约了成本。很多相对复杂的器物,部件多是分开铸造的,然后利用榫卯结构、套合方式等实现器物的整体组装。这是汉代复杂青铜器的特点。这种方式能使复杂高大的青铜器在存储时缩小占用的空间,也便于携带。

表面有密集线刻纹饰的扁壶
Bronze Hu with Thick Engraved Linear Patterns

3. 实用青铜器的别样繁荣

秦汉时期,青铜礼器属性的淡化,日常实用器类的多样化,成就了铜灯和铜镜这两个类别的繁荣。

is a characteristic of complex bronze wares from the Han Dynasty. This approach allows complex and tall bronze objects to be stored in a reduced space and to be easily carried.

博山炉一共分成五个独立的部分铸造，然后通过套合和榫卯结构完成组合
The Boshan Furnace Was Cast in Five Separate Parts, and then Assembled by Means of Socket and Mortise and Tenon Construction

3. Prosperity of Unique Practical Bronze Treasures

During the Qin and Han dynasties, the dilution of the attributes of bronze ritual objects and the diversification of the category of everyday utilitarian objects led to the prosperity of the two categories of bronze lamps and mirrors.

Bronze lamps and lanterns already had more complex designs in the Warring States Period but their overall appearance is difficult to tell because of the small number of excavations. By the time of the Qin and Han dynasties, the number of lamps excavated grew greatly and the types increased significantly, and they were unearthed in all types of tombs, indicating that bronze lamps were widely popularized. The main types are dou-shaped lamps, animal-shaped lamps, human-shaped lamps, and even branch lamps. The dou-shaped lamps are the most

青铜灯具在战国时期已经有较为复杂的设计，由于出土的数量较少，其整体面貌很难说清楚。到秦汉时，出土的灯具数量大为增长，类型也明显增多，并且各类型的墓葬中均有出土，说明青铜灯具得到了广泛普及。类型主要有豆形灯、动物形灯、人形灯、连枝灯等。豆形灯数量最多，属于简单实用类。动物形灯是汉代灯具很有趣味性的一类，通过对现实动物的模仿，加上巧妙的设计，使其形象生动、活泼可爱，增添不少生活的情调。连枝灯是仿植物枝干而成的灯具，通过枝干相互套接、搭载，完成灯体的成形，这类灯具相对比较高大，灯盏数量多，多出土于大型贵族墓葬，和贵族奢华的夜生活以及其需要的宏大场面是相匹配的。

豆形灯
Dou-shaped Bronze Lamp

铜镜在中国出现较早，最早的可追溯到齐家文化（约公元前2000—前1600年），商代和西周时期也有零星的发现，但是其实用效果很差。到了战国时代，铜镜在造型、纹饰等方面有了长足进步，很多铜镜制作十分精美。由于铜镜材料配比和当时的青铜器相近，因此其使用效果并不理想。秦汉以后，铜镜在造型、题材和合金比例上都有突破性的发展。

numerous and belong to the simple and practical category. Animal-shaped lamps were a very interesting type of lamp in the Han Dynasty and their imitation of real animals and clever design made them lively and vivid. Multi-branch lamps were made resembling the actual plant branches, which were connected and carried by the branches to complete the shaping of the lamp body. These lamps were relatively tall and numerous and have mostly been found in large noble tombs depicting grand scenes.

多枝灯
Multi-branch Bronze Lamp

Bronze mirrors appeared early in China, the earliest dating back to the Qijia culture (c. 2000-1600 BC), and were found sporadically during the Shang and Western Zhou dynasties but their practical effects were poor. By the Warring

卧羊灯
Bronze Lamp in the Shape of a Reclining Sheep

造型一改此前的平面镜面为微凸镜面，使镜面的成像有缩影效果。题材包罗万象，既有几何纹饰，又有山川河流、花草禽兽、神仙故事、人物传说等。合金比例加大了锡的比重，质地更为坚硬，使打磨后的镜面光亮程度更高，成像效果更佳。秦汉各类型墓葬均出土有铜镜，数量很多，是各阶层人群常用物品。西汉早期流行的主要是蟠螭纹镜、蟠虺纹镜、四山镜等战国时期已有的几种类型，是对此前铜镜的发展延续；西汉中期流行的主要是草叶纹镜、日光镜、星云纹镜等；西汉晚期至东汉早期主要流行博局镜，东汉中晚期流行的主要是连弧纹镜、鸟兽纹镜、四叶纹镜等。两汉是中国铜镜发展史上的第一个高峰期，题材不受限制是铜镜在这一阶段得以快速发展的重要原因，同时也是人们生活质量提高的反映。由于新的更好的能够方便映照妆容的材料迟迟没有被发现，铜镜在中国整个封建王朝时代一直持续存在，也成为唯一一个贯穿中国文明的青铜器类。

States period, bronze mirrors had made great progress in terms of shape and ornamentation, and many were very beautifully made. However, the bronze mirrors were still not ideal, because the ratio of the materials remained no difference from other bronze wares. After the Qin and Han dynasties, bronze mirrors achieved a breakthrough in shape, subject matter, and alloy ratios. The shape had changed from the previous flat mirror to a slightly convex mirror, so that the imaging of the mirror's surface had a miniature effect. The subject matter is all-encompassing, including geometric motifs, mountains, rivers, flowers, animals, stories of gods and goddesses, and legends. The alloy ratio increased in the proportion of tin and the texture was harder, making the polished mirrors shinier and more effective. Bronze mirrors were excavated from all types of tombs in the Qin and Han dynasties and there were many of them which were commonly used by people of all classes. In the early Western Han Dynasty, several types of mirrors were popular, such as the *panchi* mirror, *panhui* mirror, and *sishan* mirror, which were a continuation of the previous bronze mirrors; in the middle time of the Western Han Dynasty, the popular mirrors were mainly grass and leaf mirrors, sunlight mirrors, and star-cloud mirrors; in the late Western Han Dynasty and the early Eastern Han Dynasty, the popular mirrors were mainly *boju* mirrors, and in the middle and late Eastern Han Dynasty, the popular mirrors were mainly the mirrors with arc patterns, mirrors with bird and animal patterns, and

蟠虺纹镜
Bronze Mirror with *Panhui* Patterns

草叶纹镜
Bronze Mirror with Grass and Leaf Patterns

博局镜
Bronze Mirror with Boju Patterns

four-leaf pattern mirrors. The Western Han and Eastern Han dynasties were the first peak in the history of Chinese bronze mirrors, and the unrestricted subject matter was an important reason for the rapid development of bronze mirrors at this stage, as well as a reflection of people's improved quality of life. Due to the delay in the discovery of new and better materials, bronze mirrors continued to exist throughout imperial history and became the only bronze object that lasted throughout Chinese civilization.

鸟兽纹镜
Bronze Mirror with Bird and Animal Patterns

三、大道至简：实用与精神的并存转型

1. 朴素是秦汉青铜器的主流

说到青铜器，大多数人会将目光投向精美奇特的器物身上，这也正是商周青铜器的最大特色，然而秦汉青铜器走的是另外一条路。秦汉时期虽然也有工艺繁缛、纹饰复杂的精美器物，但数量并不多，也多属于贵族阶层的用品，不能反映秦汉青铜器的整体面貌。秦汉青铜器无论是传统礼器还是实用器，绝大部分是素面无纹饰的，即使有，也就一条弦纹或者一周宽带纹而已，造型简单的器物如此，造型复杂的也多如此。这一现象是对战国晚期开始大量出现的素面铜器的继承和延续，是青铜器走下神坛、面向大众的体现，也是青铜器从代表身份等级的礼器向日常生活用器的转折。西汉初年，社会刚从动荡中安定下来，物资匮乏，国家急需休养生息，恢复生机。朝堂之上黄老无为而治的思想占据着主导地位，因而从工官作坊出来的素面青铜器本身就反映了庙堂的主导思想，其他制作青铜器的地方效而仿之也就顺理成章了。承载着礼仪属性

素面铜甑釜

Bronze Zeng and Fu Cauldron with a Plain Surface

III. The Way to Simplicity: Practical and Spiritual Coexistence

1. Plainness as the Mainstream of the Qin and Han Bronze Treasures

When it comes to bronze objects, most people focus on the exquisite and peculiar art, which is the most striking feature of Shang and Zhou bronze wares. However, the Qin and Han bronze wares took a different path. Although there were also exquisite objects with elaborate craftsmanship and complex ornamentation during the Qin and Han dynasties, they were few in number, mostly belonged to the noble class, and did not reflect the overall characteristics of the Qin and Han bronze wares. These objects, whether traditional, ceremonial, or practical, are plain in decoration or feature a simple string pattern or broadband pattern. This was the result of the long-term dilution and popularization of bronze objects that had taken place since the Eastern Zhou. In the early years of the Western Han Dynasty, society had just settled down from the battles and conflicts of the Qin unification and materials had become scarce. As the society was dominated by the Yellow Emperor's and the Taoist philosophy of doing-nothing against nature, it was only logical that the plain bronze wares from the workshops of the government reflected the dominant idea of the royal court and that other places making bronze wares would follow suit. The bronze ritual

素面铜灶

Bronze Stove with a Plain Surface

的青铜礼器尚且素面，实用青铜器更没有必要去多加装饰。不少青铜器是通过铸造文字或者凿刻文字来表达器物的部分内涵，装饰华丽的纹饰也就可有可无了。从实用角度来看，大部分实用器使用频率较高，如釜、甑等炊煮用具，耳杯、樽、钘等酒器，盆、洗等水器，一般都造型简单，不做复杂的纹饰修饰，可能也有实用至上、清洗方便的用意。

2. 神仙思想、吉祥如意是汉代青铜器精神层面的特点

秦汉初期，传统礼器无论是造型还是纹饰，皆受东周礼制文化影响。汉武帝罢黜百家、独尊儒术的政策，逐渐成为汉代的统一思想，为形成汉代青铜器的精神内涵奠定了基础。礼器本身或者消失，或者转向实用器物。

西汉早期，贵族阶层受战国时期长生不老、神仙思想的影响，也在追求通过寻访术士、炼丹修行等方式获得永生。新兴实用青铜器因不受礼器用途的束缚，神仙思想题材的纹饰开始得到发展，这是西汉王朝礼制青铜器精神内涵以外的另一种思想在青铜器上的体现。和神仙生活、长生不老密切关联的云气纹、青龙、白虎、朱雀、玄武、青山、神兽等纹饰题材逐渐丰满生动。整个社会流行着天人感应和羽化升仙的思想，尤其在樽、博山炉等器物上得到反映。樽是酒器，酒能助兴，让人有飘飘欲仙的感觉，更能帮助饮酒者进入幻想的空间。博山炉是熏器，烟雾缥缈、清香缕缕的氛围又很贴切神仙的生活。在不同功能的器物上装饰合适的隐喻题材，既能丰富器物的文化内涵，也能体现铸造工匠的艺术水平。带有这类装饰题材的铜器，往往制作精美，来源于豪门大族，羽化成仙这样的美事好像只是王公贵胄才有资格，至于平民百姓，活着尚且不易，哪还有得道升仙的想法。

公元25年，刘秀称帝，迁都洛阳，开启东汉王朝。这个时候，青铜器的纹饰和铭文开始不同于西汉，生活化现象更加明显。战国至秦汉以来高级贵族追求的长生不老、神仙生活并没有因为身份的高贵就得以

vessels which carried ritual properties were still plain and there was no need to decorate practical bronze wares. Many of the bronze objects were cast or chiseled to express part of the connotation of the object and decorative ornaments were also dispensable. From a practical point of view, most of the utilitarian wares were made more frequently such as cooking utensils like *fu* and *zeng*, drinking vessels such as ear cups, *zun* bottles and *xing* flasks, and water vessels such as *pen* and *xi* washbasins.

2. Pursuit of the Heavenly and Good Fortune in the Han Dynasty

In the early Qin and Han dynasties, traditional ceremonial vessels were influenced by the ritual culture of the Eastern Zhou Dynasty, both in shape and decoration. Emperor Wu's policy of dismissing the hundred schools and respecting only Confucianism gradually became the unifying idea of the Han Dynasty, laying the foundation for the formation of the spiritual connotations of Han Dynasty bronze wares. The ritual objects themselves either disappeared or shifted to practical objects.

In the early Western Han Dynasty, the noble class, influenced by the ideas of immortality during the Warring States Period, was also pursuing immortality through visits to sorcerers and by indulging in alchemical practices. The emerging bronze wares employed ornamentation of divine immortality. The ornamental motifs such as cloud and air patterns, blue dragon, white tiger, rosefinch, tortoise, blue mountain and divine beast, which were closely related to the life of the gods and immortality, were gradually fleshed out. The idea of celestial induction and ascension to immortality was popular throughout society, especially reflected in such objects as bottles and Boshan stoves. The bottle was a drinking vessel, and the wine helped to make people feel like they were floating to immortality, and was more likely to help the drinker enter the space of fantasy. The Boshan stove was a smoker and the atmosphere of misty smoke and fragrance was associated with the gods. Decorating different functional objects with appropriate metaphorical motifs could enrich the cultural connotation of the objects as well as reflect the artistic level of the foundry artisans. Bronze objects with such decorative motifs, often beautifully crafted, came from the gentry, and such a beautiful thing as a feathered immortal seems to be qualified only for the princes and nobles. The

实现。西汉末年的社会动乱给百姓带来的更多是困苦,人们迫切需要在现实世界中得到安定、财富和权利。儒家思想在朝堂上地位的巩固,结合百姓面对生活的需求、贴近现实的期盼,使得富贵安康、吉祥如意逐渐成了主流思想。像鱼、羊、鹭、钱币等纹饰纷纷出现在青铜器上,并配"长宜子孙""宜子孙""宜侯王""大吉""大吉羊""君至三公"等吉语铸铭构成装饰,表达了这时期人们祈求年年有余、富贵安康、吉祥如意的思想,是精神需求在器物上的表现。

鱼纹铜洗
Bronze Xi Washbasin with Fish Patterns

鱼纹铜洗内底纹饰
The Fish Pattern on the Inner Surface of the Bronze Xi Washbasin

ordinary people who were struggling for subsistence and survival had in fact no slight idea of ascending to immortality.

云龙纹盘
Bronze Plate with Cloud and Thunder Patterns

四神羽人铜樽
Bronze Zun with Four Feathered Men

148　第三章　百花齐放——秦汉帝国时代河南青铜艺术的转型之路

龙首铜熨斗
Bronze Iron with a Dragon-head-shaped Handle

熨斗底部"货泉"钱币
The Huoquan Coin Pattern at the Bottom of the Bronze Iron

"大吉"铜钟
Bronze Bell with Characters Da Ji

The Western Han began to experience social turmoil. In 25 A.D., Liu Xiu became the emperor, and moved the capital to Luoyang, starting the Eastern Han Dynasty. At this time, the ornamentations and inscriptions on the bronze objects began to differ from those of the Western Han in the more obvious preference for the earthly life. The noble people's pursuit for immortality and divine life since the Warring States to the Qin and Han dynasties were never realized as they expected. The social turmoil of the late Western Han Dynasty brought hardship to the people, who desperately needed stability, wealth, and power. Confucianism had become the state ideology by this time and it combined with the people's secular preoccupations, elevating wealth, prosperity, and good fortune to a dominant place in bronze art. Fish, sheep, herons, coins, and other motifs appeared on bronze objects. This was an expression of people's desire to have a good year with good fortune.

鎏金云纹耳杯底部"宜子孙"

Characters Yi Zi Sun on the Bottom of the Gilt Bronze Ear Cup with Cloud Patterns

3. 私营作坊是青铜器转型的推手

汉代铸铜机构可分为官营、私营和官私合营三种形式。官营机构中，一类是由汉王朝中央直接管辖的，如少府、上林苑等；一类是由中央任命管理官吏的工官作坊，设在郡县；还有一类是县或侯国的官府手工业部门。官营制器业规模很大，产品主要供宫廷和各级官府使用。

青铜器铸造中的私营作坊在战国时期才逐渐发展起来，汉初时还不成熟。西汉早期地方贵族、侯国除了可以获得赋税财富，还有权开采铜矿，铸造货币和器物。这时候的家族势力有相当一部分是战国至秦延续下来的，对此前时代的青铜器还存在着眷恋，这也是汉初传统青铜礼器得以延续战国风格的重要原因，同时也为新兴实用青铜器的繁荣打下了基础。汉武帝时，将铸币权收归中央而实行禁铜政策后，私营作坊萎缩，官制青铜器制作则更注重上层社会的思想追求和集体意识。进入东汉，随着政策的松动、庄园经济的发达，豪强地主林立，私营作坊开始日益壮大，各级工官逐渐退出青铜器生产领域，青铜器基本为私营作坊所造。成为商品的青铜器为了迎合人们的心理期许和生活需求，又想扩大影响，不仅在器类上不断丰富，而且在纹饰上也多用吉祥如意、富贵安康的题材，并配有吉祥用语、作坊名、产地等，这些共同构成青铜器全新的内涵。生产经营方式及器物纹饰、类型的演变，都充分说明了青铜器在汉代的走向，即由宫廷贵族之室进入寻常百姓之家，由身份等级象征的礼器转变为实用的器物。原本掌握在高层贵族手中的铜料资源、铸造工匠以及其所制作的青铜器，是需要通过立功、赏赐、掳掠等方式才可以获得的，是神秘的、荣耀的、尊贵的。而当青铜器成为商品，只要付钱就可以得到的时候，青铜器就和其他商品一样，不再有更多的附加意义了，所有的种类以及施加的纹饰都要满足购买者的需求这一基本条件，更要考虑如何迎合购买者的想法。针对不同的购买群体，极尽奢华的青铜器流入豪强地主之家，物美价廉的则是寻常百姓的首选。

3. Private Workshops as the Driving Force for Bronze Transformation

Han Dynasty copper casting institutions could be divided into three types: those run by the government, those run by private workshops, and those run by both. Among the government-run institutions, the first category was directly under the jurisdiction of the central Han Dynasty, such as Shaofu, Shanglingyuan. The second category was appointed by the central government to manage officials' workshops, located in counties. The third category was the official handicraft department of counties or marquis states. The official ware-making industry was very large, and the products were mainly for the use of the palace and officialdom at all levels.

Private workshops in bronze casting were only gradually developed during the Warring States Period and were immature in the early Han. In addition to access to tax wealth, local nobles and marquis states in the early Western Han period had the right to mine copper and cast currency and wares. A significant portion of the family power at this time was carried over from the Warring States to the Qin, and there was still an attachment to the bronze ware of previous eras, which was an important reason why the traditional bronze rituals of the early Han were able to continue the Warring States style while also laying the foundation for the prosperity of the emerging practical bronze ware. When the Western Han emperor returned the power of coinage to the central government and imposed a bronze ban, private workshops shrank and the production of official bronze vessels became more focused on the ideological pursuits and collective consciousness of the upper classes. In the Eastern Han Dynasty, with the loosening of the policy, the development of the estate economy and the establishment of powerful landlords, private workshops began to grow, and the government officials at all levels gradually withdrew from the production of bronze wares, which were basically made by private workshops. In order to meet people's psychological expectations and needs, and to expand their influence, the bronze objects became commodities, not only in terms of types of wares but also in terms of ornamentation with auspicious themes including auspicious phrases, names of workshops and places of origin. This constituted a new connotation of the bronze wares. The evolution of production methods, ornaments, and types of objects fully illustrates the trend of bronze wares during the Han Dynasty from the rooms of

第三章 百花齐放——秦汉帝国时代河南青铜艺术的转型之路

线刻纹鎏金羽人铜座
Bronze Stand in the Shape of a Feathered Man

the court nobility to the homes of ordinary people, from ritual objects as symbols of status and rank to practical objects. Originally in the hands of the high nobility, the bronze resources, foundry craftsmen and the bronze wares they made were mysterious, glorious and honored. They could only be obtained through merit, reward, and captivity. When bronze became a commodity that could be obtained by paying for it, it no longer had any more meaning than any other commodity and all the types and the ornaments had to meet the basic condition of the purchaser's needs, and consideration had to be paid to the purchaser's demands. For different groups of purchasers, the most luxurious bronze objects went to the houses of powerful landowners, while the more affordable ones were preferred by the common people.

鎏金铜樽
Gilt Bronze Zun Vessel

四、历史选择：青铜器的没落

　　青铜器传入中原以后，从工具类向仿陶铜容器迈进，在这一过程中，逐渐被赋予了更多的内涵，成为贵族阶层特有的物品以及身份等级的象征。商周时期，通过附加复杂的纹饰和上层社会拥有的文字，青铜器的内涵越来越丰富，成为固定社会阶层、彰显贵族优越感的神秘器物。也正是因为它属于上层社会，这阶层的人群拥有大量财力、物力、人力，因此成就了中国青铜器商末周初的第一个高峰。到东周时，诸侯国实力逐渐强大，开始对青铜器所赋予的身份等级产生怀疑，并于行动上僭越，青铜器早期精神内涵开始被打破。诸侯国国力的强盛加上百家争鸣的时代背景，为青铜器走上欣欣向荣的第二个高峰奠定了基础。此后青铜器开始沿着没落的方向前进。

　　秦汉时期，人们向往长生不老、神仙生活、富贵安康，青铜礼器地位越来越低，区分身份等级不再靠青铜礼器。大量的新兴青铜器失去了原有的神秘感、崇敬感。随着经济社会的发展，私营青铜器作坊壮大，青铜器成为商品进入寻常百姓家。秦至汉初，对战国时期列国文化思想的传承，使传统青铜礼器有一定的地域性，这种地域性有更多的原诸侯国文化因素。但在各诸侯国长期的政治、经济、文化交流中，地域性特征越来越模糊，原来某个诸侯国在自己统治地域内使用的青铜器，开始突破地域的限制，在更广泛的空间内流传。随着秦逐步统一天下，如具有强烈秦文化因素的蒜头壶，便随着秦人征程散播到其统治下的全国各地。秦汉一统，强大的中央集权实现了思想、文化上的趋同和民族的融合，传统青铜器和实用青铜器突破了地域的因素逐步走向一致，除边远地区部分类别的青铜器有较为强烈的地域特征外，更广阔的疆域内使用的青铜器在种类、造型上则具有相对的普遍性。

IV. Historical Choices: The Decline of China's Bronze Culture

After bronze was introduced to the Central Plains, it progressed from a tool to pottery-like bronze containing vessels, and in the process was gradually given more connotations, becoming an object unique to the noble class and a symbol of status and rank. During the Shang and Zhou periods, by attaching complex ornaments and texts owned by the upper class, bronze became richer and richer in connotation, becoming a mysterious object that fixed the social class and manifested the superiority of the nobility. It was also because it belonged to the upper class, a class of people who possessed a great deal of financial, material and human resources, that it achieved the first peak of Chinese bronze ware in the late Shang and early Zhou dynasties. By the time of the Eastern Zhou Dynasty, the vassal states grew stronger and began to question the status hierarchy conferred by the bronze, and to overstep it in their actions, and the early spiritual connotations of the bronze began to be broken. The strength of the vassal states, combined with the background of a hundred schools of thought, laid the foundation for the second peak of bronze to flourish. Thereafter bronze began to move in the direction of decline.

During the Qin and Han dynasties, people aspired to immortality, divine life, wealth and well-being, the status of bronze rituals became reduced and the distinction between status classes no longer depended on bronze rituals. A large number of emerging bronze vessels lost their original mystery and reverence. With the development of the economy and society, private bronze workshops grew and bronze became a commodity in ordinary people's homes. From Qin to early Han, the inheritance of cultural ideas from the Warring States Period made the traditional bronze rituals have a certain regional character, and this regional character had more cultural factors of the original vassal states. However, in the long-term political, economic and cultural exchanges among the vassal states, the regional character became increasingly blurred, and the bronze wares originally used by a certain vassal state in its own ruling territory began to break through the limits of the region and circulate in a wider space. As the Qin gradually unified

秦汉一统后，社会趋于稳定，物质资料迅速丰盈。物品间的交换需要大量的统一货币来支撑和结算，加上初期时地方也可铸造货币，大量的铜资源被占用，青铜器用材受到挤压。铁的出现及大量使用，使青铜工具和兵器逐渐退出了历史舞台。战国时期开始流行的漆器，随着秦汉时期漆树大面积种植，漆器产品增多，其绚丽的色彩，深受高级贵族喜爱，承担了一部分青铜器物的职能，也替代了一部分物品，比如耳杯、盒、盘等。贵族之间宴饮活动更多选择漆器，这和当时贵族之间的审美取向有一定的关系。原始瓷器经过近两千年的发展，到汉代实现了突破。同时，质地坚硬、釉面光洁、色泽稳定的青瓷出现了，挤占了大多数实用青铜器的功能。而玉器在汉代礼仪方面地位的进一步提升，也使青铜礼器的仪礼功能逐渐被淡化了。总之，秦汉之后，由于种种原因，只有零星青铜器类还有所发展、使用，但已撑不起青铜器这一大类。青铜器的没落，是历史的选择。

综上所述，夏代是中国进入青铜时代的初期，铸造业还不发达，但鼎、爵等青铜容器的出现，是生产技术上的一次飞跃。商代青铜器从制式到纹样都反映了那个时代的风貌。各种各样的盛酒器、温酒器、饮酒器，反映了贵族阶层极尽奢侈的生活；令人印象深刻的狰狞的兽面纹，给人一种神秘、庄严之感，象征着统治阶级雄踞社会之上的威严、权势。两周列国的青铜器，继商代青铜器的狞厉与辉煌后，走过了一个从礼制森严、质朴庄重到风姿各异、标新立异的发展过程。随着西周末期崇德、疑天思想的兴起，理性的、现实的观念日益滋长，青铜器皿也失去了神圣的光圈和威慑力量。到春秋中后期，纹饰、造型向灵巧多变和实用发展。到战国晚期，西周以来的礼制已不复存在，贵族墓多以仿铜陶礼器随葬，此时，人们的注意力转移到新兴的铁器和漆器制作上，鼎盛一时的青铜文化便由盛而衰。秦汉的大一统，实现了思想自上而下的逐步统一，反映在青铜器上的地域差异越来越小。现实生活中除了贵族阶层使用的部分青铜器是精美奢华的，其他多数是朴素无纹的，是实用至上理

the country, the garlic pots, for example, with strong Qin cultural elements, spread throughout the country under the Qin's rule with the Qin's expedition. With the unification of the Qin and Han dynasties, the powerful centralization of power brought about the convergence of ideas and cultures and the integration of nationalities, and the traditional and practical bronze vessels broke through the geographical factors and gradually became standardized.

After the unification of the Qin and Han dynasties, society became more stable and material resources were abundant. The exchange of goods required a large amount of uniform currency to support and settle, and with the fact that localities could also mint money in the early days, a large amount of copper resources were taken up and the material for bronze tools was squeezed. The emergence of iron and its massive use caused bronze tools and weapons to gradually recede from the stage of history. Lacquerware, which became popular during the Warring States Period, increased in number as lacquer trees were planted on a large scale during the Qin and Han dynasties. With its brilliant colors, lacquerware was loved by high-ranking nobles and assumed some of the functions of bronze objects and also replaced some items, such as ear cups, boxes, and plates. The greater choice of lacquerware for banquets among the nobility had something to do with the aesthetic orientation among the nobility at the time. After nearly two thousand years of development, primitive porcelain achieved a breakthrough in the Han Dynasty. At the same time, celadon, with its hard texture, glossy glaze and stable color, emerged, crowding out the function of most practical bronze wares. The further elevation of the status of jade in Han rituals also caused the ceremonial function of bronze rituals to be gradually diluted. In short, after the Qin and Han dynasties, for various reasons, only a few bronze wares were developed and used, the inadequacy of which did not deserve a category as they used to. The decline of bronze was therefore the choice of history.

To sum up, the Xia Dynasty was the beginning of the Bronze Age in China, and the foundry industry was not yet developed, but the appearance of bronze vessels such as *ding* and *jue* was a leap forward in production technology. Bronze objects of the Shang Dynasty reflected the style of that era from the style to the pattern. The various kinds of wine containers, wine warmers, and drinking vessels reflected the extremely luxurious life of the noble class; the impressive

念的反映。精神生活上追求羽化成仙、长生不老、富贵安康,青铜器纹饰也就多为相关的题材。青铜器商品化后,神秘色彩消失,功用逐渐被其他材质的器物所取代。

hideous animal face pattern gave a sense of mystery and solemnity, symbolizing the majesty and power of the ruling class over society. The bronze objects of the Western Zhou and Eastern Zhou dynasties, following the deterrent and carnivalesque brilliance in the Shang Dynasty, had gone through a process of development from strict hierarchy and solemn simplicity to various styles and original novelty. With the rise of virtue and skepticism about Heaven at the end of the Western Zhou Dynasty, rational and realistic ideas grew and the bronze wares lost their sacred aperture and intimidating power. By the middle to late Spring and Autumn Period, ornamentation and modelling developed towards dexterity, versatility, and practicality. By the late Warring States Period, the ritual system that had existed since the Western Zhou no longer existed and the nobles' tombs were mostly buried with imitation bronze pottery ritual vessels. At that point, attention shifted to the emerging production of iron and lacquerware and the heyday of bronze culture went from prosperity to decline. The great unification of the Qin and Han dynasties brought about a gradual unification of ideas from the top down, and the regional differences reflected in the bronze wares became fewer. In real life, except for some of the bronze objects used by the noble class, most of them were exquisite and luxurious but most of the others were simple and without patterns, reflecting practicality. In spiritual life, as to the pursuit of immortality, wealth, and well-being, the bronze ornaments were mostly related themes. After the commercialization of bronze, the mysterious color disappeared and its place was gradually assumed by other material objects.

第四章

承传不衰——宋以来对青铜文明
的追求与重建

Chapter 4

Rebirth: Bronze's Comeback Under the Song, Ming,

and Qing Dynasties

一、青铜礼制在宋、明、清三代的复兴

周代所制定的典章制度及其礼制文化,对中国传统文化产生了深远的影响。中国的传统文化与文明正是以"礼"为核心。中原这片沃土上所铸就的青铜文明,是在融合南北、交流东西的过程中不断进行文化碰撞的产物。夏商周时期礼制形成、完善,而最终被僭越的政治背景,决定了夏商周时期中国的青铜文化走过了和谐有序、等级分明、中和融通的道路。秦汉以后,尽管朝代不断更迭、物质原料日益更新,但历代统治者无一不宗法周礼并视其为治国之根本。

宋、明、清三代,皇权出于统治的需要,曾重建屡经创伤且早以崩坏的周礼制度,在中国大地上掀起了三次复兴青铜礼制文明的浪潮。这种复兴青铜文明,是通过研究古代遗物与文献记载来进行的。

以青铜器为研究对象是宋代新兴的金石学的重要内容之一,金石学是以研究青铜器及其铭文和石刻文字等的心得去校正文献、经书的治学方法。研究古代青铜器与石刻之所以受到学者的重视,一方面是因为金石之学不仅可以证经补史,而且有助于复原古礼,适应了北宋王朝鼓励经学、巩固统治秩序之需要。另一方面,金石之学有实证研究色彩,为当时代表进步的史学与文字学发展趋势的学者所推重。北宋时造纸、印刷与墨拓技术得到空前提高,也为金石学的发展创造了物质条件。一时间,金石学名家辈出,著述颇丰,得以传承至今的论著有《宣和博古图》《金石录》《考古图》等。

明清时期,金石学的研究则局限于考释铭文、收集资料、判定时代等方面。当时的文人墨客、达官贵人以收藏有三代青铜器为荣,是能踏入当时金石学文化圈的重要标志。伴随着文化和思想的需求,出现了仿古彝器,除了青铜材质,在玉、陶、瓷等其他材质上也多有仿青铜器造型的出现。这一现象,并不是单纯的仿造,而是对夏、商、周三代礼乐

I. Revival of Bronze Rituals in the Song, Ming, and Qing Dynasties

The rules and regulations established during the Zhou Dynasty and its ritual culture have had a profound impact on traditional Chinese culture. The traditional culture and civilization of China were centered on the rites. The bronze civilization forged in the fertile soil of the Central Plains was the product of a constant cultural collision in the process of fusion of the North and the South and exchange between the East and the West. The political background of the formation and perfection of the ritual system during the Xia, Shang, and Zhou periods, and its dismantling, determined the harmonious and orderly, hierarchical, neutral and harmonious path of Chinese bronze culture throughout the early periods. After the Qin and Han dynasties, despite the change of dynasties and the renewal of materials, all rulers of successive dynasties followed the Zhou rites and regarded them as the basis of governance.

During the Song, Ming, and Qing dynasties, the imperial power rebuilt the repeatedly traumatized and long-destroyed Zhou ritual system out of the need to rule, setting off three waves of revival of the bronze ritual civilization in China. This renaissance was carried out through the study of the ancient relics and documents.

Bronze was one of the important elements of the emerging Jinshi epigraphy research during the Song Dynasty. The idea was to study bronze and stone inscriptions and make corrections on the earlier documents and Confucian classics. The research was vital because the study of ancient bronze and stone tablets could not only verify the history but help restore the ancient rites to meet the needs of the Northern Song Dynasty to use scripture to consolidate the ruling order. In the Northern Song Dynasty, paper making, printing, and ink topography technology had been highly improved, thus providing foundation for the development of Jinshi epigraphy. At that time, there appeared quite a lot of famous scholars, producing an abundance of writings or treatises in this field including *Xuanhe Bogu Tu*, *Jinshi Lu* and *Kaogu Tu*, which are still often referred to even today.

制度的追求与重建。

　　随着考古学传入中国，在结合中国实际情况的过程中科学、有序地发展壮大，越来越多的青铜器面世，夏、商、周时期的各类有效信息越来越丰富，在中国考古学者和日、韩、欧美学者的不断研究探索中，中国青铜器的面貌越来越清晰，中国青铜器背后的文化礼仪也越来越丰满。这一过程，让中国人了解了自己的祖先如何在这片广袤的土地上生根发芽，发展壮大，如何了解自然、利用自然、与自然和谐共存，进而实现中国人心中的文化自信。科学有效的文化信息不断叠加于青铜器上，让走进博物馆的人们不仅看到了祖先曾经创造的集智慧、技术与艺术于一体的青铜器，而且能联想到其背后所蕴含的让中华文明经久不衰的本质——不断追求与重建下延绵不断、传承有序的礼仪文化。

During the Ming and Qing dynasties, the study of Jinshi was limited to the examination and interpretation of inscriptions, the collection of data, and other bureaucratic needs of the era. The literati and dignitaries took pride in having a collection of bronze objects from the three generations, an important sign of being able to step into the cultural circle of Jinshi research. Along with the demand for culture and thought came the emergence of imitation ritual vessels, and in addition to bronze, there were many imitations of bronze shapes in other materials such as jade, pottery, and porcelain. This phenomenon was not a mere imitation but a pursuit and reconstruction of the ritual and music system of the Xia, Shang, and Zhou dynasties.

With the introduction of archaeology into China, Jinshi research has developed and grown scientifically and orderly. As the discoveries of bronze artifacts appeared, more and more information about the Xia, Shang, and Zhou periods has accumulated, providing a better outline of Chinese bronze wares and the cultural rituals behind them because of the continuous research and exploration of Chinese archaeologists and Japanese, Korean, European and American scholars. This process has enabled the Chinese to understand how their ancestors took root and developed in this vast land, how they understood nature, utilized it, and coexisted in harmony with it, thus realizing the cultural confidence in the hearts of the Chinese. The scientific and valid cultural information was constantly superimposed on the bronze so that when people enter the museums today, not only do they see the wisdom, technology, and art of the bronze once but they can also associate it with the essence that makes Chinese civilization endure – the continuous pursuit and reconstruction of an unbroken and orderly ritual culture.

二、以鼎为核心的青铜文化特质

礼见于器,最典型的莫过于鼎。鼎在中国历史上沿用时间极长,从新石器时代距今约8000年前开始一直到现在还在使用,集唯一性、代表性、历史性、艺术性于一身。另一方面,鼎在长期的使用过程中还具备了诸多文化属性,是器以藏礼、由器而道的典型物证。

鼎,起源于民之炊食。三足陶质鼎最早可以追溯到公元前6000年左右。三足铜质鼎则最早出现于夏代的偃师二里头。其后至商周时期,青铜鼎得到了迅猛发展,并被赋予了思想内涵,对此后中华文明的发展产生了长远深厚的影响。

传说中鼎的铸造始自于黄帝。《史记·孝武本纪》记载:"皇帝采首山铜,铸鼎于荆山下。"由于年代久远,目前的考古资料也无从证实其真实性,故只能以传说说之。相对于鼎形器物的出现并流传,鼎的文字出现则要相对晚一些,这与汉字的发明有着直接的关系。甲骨文出现之前,鼎是以什么样的文字符号或图画来表现的我们无法知道,但是在甲骨文时代,鼎字常出现于甲骨文中。其象形的文字形态多作为占卜的"贞"用。如此来看,由鼎形器物演化而来的象形文字鼎字本身是代表了一种向天或神问询吉凶的思想。那么说明,此时鼎本身可能是具有这样的思想内涵的。

商周青铜器中许多器类的定名需要文献、实物与器物本身自铭相结合来加以考证,而鼎在这方面则几乎不存在这样的问题。除了鼎在中华文明中的特殊意义使得大众都对其有一个传承有序的认识外,鼎类器物和鼎的文字在商周时期就已经完成了两者的统一。即当文字从甲骨上转移到青铜器上时,自铭器实现了鼎字和鼎类器物的统一。当然,这一问题只是针对今人对古代器物的认识上存在的问题,而当时的人们是不存在文字和器物不一致的情况的。

II. Unique Traits of Ding as the Core of the Bronze Culture

Rites are found in vessels, and there is nothing more representative of it than the *ding*. The *ding* has been used for a very long time in Chinese history, starting from the Neolithic Age about 8,000 years ago to its use at the present time, combining uniqueness, representativeness, historical significance, and artistic beauty. On the other hand, the *ding* has also acquired many cultural attributes during its long-term use, and is typical of the rituals hidden in the vessel and the conveyance of thoughts through the vessel.

The *ding* originated from cooking. The three-legged ceramic tripod can be traced back to about 6000 B.C. The three-legged bronze tripod first appeared in Erlitou, Yanshi, during the Xia Dynasty. Later, during the Shang and Zhou dynasties, the bronze *ding* developed rapidly and was endowed with ideological connotations, which had a long and profound influence on the development of Chinese civilization thereafter.

Legend has it that the casting of the *ding* began with the Yellow Emperor. In *Shi Ji*, it is written that "the emperor took copper from stones and made the *ding* at the bottom of Jingshan Mountain." Due to its age, there is no way to confirm its authenticity with the current archaeological data, so we can only speak of it as a legend. Compared with the appearance and circulation of ding-shaped objects, the appearance of *ding* writing is relatively late and is directly related to the invention of Chinese characters. It is not known what kind of characters or drawings were used to represent the *ding* before the appearance of the oracle bone script, but in the oracle bone era, the character for *ding* often appeared in the script. Its hieroglyphic form was mostly used as a "Zhen" for divination. In this way, the pictograph *ding*, which evolved from a ding-shaped object, represents the idea of asking Heaven or the gods about good fortune. This suggests that the *ding* itself may have had such connotations at this time.

The naming of many of the Shang and Zhou bronze wares requires a combination of documents, objects, and the inscriptions on the wares themselves, whereas the *ding* has few such problems. In addition to its special significance

汉字的形成，以及汉字载体的变化，对鼎文化的传播具有深远的意义。也是除了鼎本身所附含的文化、思想外，能够实现鼎文化对中华文化具有长远影响的重要条件。这一点具体地表现在早期文化典籍对鼎的记载上。《左传·宣公三年》记载，鼎在铸造之初，确实承载了"协于上下，以承天休"的使命，拥有鼎就是拥有这种能力或者权力的象征。但随着夏、商、周朝代的更迭，后世人们总会总结前朝失国的经验教训，于是逐步认识到一个朝代是否能够长盛不衰，关键不在于其是否拥有能够象征能力与权力的鼎本身，而在于统治者是否有德。至此，鼎当初附含的思想得到了进一步的延伸，从拥有代表国家政权象征的鼎就能拥有统治国家的权力发展到统治者不仅要拥有鼎，更重要的是要有鼎"协于上下，以承天休"的德。这也正是鼎之所以能够成为中华文明重要象征的原因。其已不再是单纯意义上的一种器物，而是成为国家政权有德者具之的象征。保存至今的大量史学典籍记载了很多关于发现铜鼎的事件，其所要传递的信息是因为统治者"德之休明"，所以发现了铜鼎，便是"天所命也"。

秦汉以来，鼎一方面在宗教、祭祀等场合继续存在，另一方面主要转化成盛食器、容器以及鼎形香炉之类。历代执政者依据先秦鼎彝进行制作与创新，正是在这种仿制与追摩中，鼎逐渐完成了文化符号的转化。鼎从8000多年前开始出现，经过数千年的演变，从生活器具到权力表征、礼制用器，逐渐上升为文化符号，其演变过程不仅是一种器皿的变化，更是一种文化与精神的传承。"一言九鼎""鼎力相助""革故鼎新"已经深深植根于我们的传统道德、传统文化中。直至今日，每逢重要场合与盛大活动，我们多喜欢铸鼎来纪念。从世纪宝鼎、香港宝鼎到民族团结宝鼎，鼎这一古老的器物被赋予了新的时代意义。

in Chinese civilization, which gave the public an orderly understanding of its inheritance, the unification of the *ding* objects and texts was already accomplished during the Shang and Zhou periods. That is, when the writing was transferred from the oracle bones to the bronze objects, the unification of the *ding* characters and the *ding*-like objects was realized by the self-inscribed vessels. Of course, this issue is only directed against the problems that exist in today's knowledge of ancient artifacts while people at that time did not have inconsistency between words and artifacts.

The formation of Chinese characters, and the changes in their carriers, have profound significance for the spread of the *ding* culture. It was also an important condition that enabled the *ding* culture to have a long-term impact on Chinese culture, in addition to the culture and ideas attached to the *ding* itself. This is specifically shown by the records of *ding* in early cultural texts. According to *Zuo Zhuan: Lord Xuan 3(BCE)*, when the *ding* was first cast, it had the mission of "harmonizing the upper and lower in order to link with Heaven", and the possession of the *ding* was a symbol of having such a power or right. However, as the dynasties of Xia, Shang, and Zhou changed, later generations always summed up the lessons learned from the loss of the previous dynasties and gradually realized that the key to the longevity of a dynasty did not lie in the possession of the *ding* itself, which symbolized power and authority, but in the virtue of the ruler. Thus, the idea attached to the *ding* was further extended, from a symbol of state power, to a symbol of having the power to rule the state, to a common belief that the ruler must not only possess the *ding*, but more importantly, he must bear the virtues of the *ding* to "harmonize with the upper and lower in order to link with Heaven". This is the reason why *ding* became an important symbol of Chinese civilization. It was no longer a mere object, but a symbol of the virtuous person in the state power. A large number of historical texts have been preserved to date, recording the discovery of the *ding* vessels, all of which express the same message that the discovery of all the *ding* vessels was made possible because the rulers were bearers of virtues, and they were all "ordained by Heaven".

Since the Qin and Han dynasties, the *ding* has continued to exist in religious and ritual contexts, but on the other hand, it has been transformed into a food vessel, a container, and a *ding*-shaped incense burner. Successive rulers made

世纪宝鼎
Shi Ji Bao Ding Cauldron

为庆贺联合国 50 华诞，中华人民共和国于 1995 年 10 月 21 日在联合国总部，向联合国赠送一尊重达 1.5 吨的青铜巨鼎——世纪宝鼎。这件鼎高 2.1 米，寓意 21 世纪；鼎座高 50 厘米，象征联合国成立 50 周年；共装饰有 56 条夔龙，代表中华人民共和国由 56 个民族组成，都是龙的传人。鼎内有"铸赠世纪宝鼎，庆贺联合国五十华诞"的铭文。鼎作为一种重要礼器，象征着团结、统一和权威，是代表和平、发展、昌盛的祥物。

香港宝鼎是中国对香港恢复行使主权的见证。鼎高 1.997 米，口径 1.68 米，连底座总重 7 吨，现位于香港大屿山"天坛大佛"入口处。鼎内刻铸铭文"定鼎铭志，庆贺香港回归祖国"。座分上下两层。上座高 0.71 米，即为香港回归祖国的具体时日——7 月 1 日，呈八角状，上饰青铜龙麟 56 片，象征香港回归到有 56 个民族组成的祖国大家庭。上座正面铸鼎名：香港宝鼎。背面铸署名，另外六面分别为：一国两制，港人治

and innovated on the basis of the pre-Qin ding, and it was in this imitation that the *ding* gradually completed its transformation into a cultural symbol. Since its appearance more than 8,000 years ago, the *ding* had evolved from a household utensil to a symbol of power and ritual, gradually rising to a cultural symbol; its evolution not only being a change of vessels, but also a cultural and spiritual heritage. The Chinese idioms "yi yan jiu ding", "ding li xiang zhu" and "ge gu ding xin" have been deeply rooted in our traditional morality and traditional culture. To this day, we like to cast *ding* to commemorate every important occasion and grand event. From the Shi Ji Bao Ding cauldron, the Hong Kong Bao Ding cauldron to the National Unity Ding cauldron, this ancient artifact has been given a new meaning in the new era of time.

To celebrate the fiftieth birthday of the United Nations, the People's Republic of China presented to the United Nations, at United Nations Headquarters on 21 October 1995, a huge bronze *ding* cauldron weighing 1.5 tons—the Shi Ji Bao Ding caudron. The *ding* is 2.1 meters high, signifying the twenty-first century; its base is 50 centimeters high, symbolizing the fiftieth anniversary of the United Nations; it is decorated with 56 *kui* dragons, representing 56 ethnic groups of the People's Republic of China, all of whom are traditionally called descendants of the dragon. The inner side of the *ding* cauldron bears the inscriptions in Chinese meaning "The *ding* is made to celebrate the 50th birthday of the United Nations". As an important ritual instrument, the *ding* symbolizes unity and authority and is an auspicious object representing peace, development, and prosperity.

The Hong Kong Bao Ding cauldron is a testimony of China's resumption of sovereignty over Hong Kong. It is 1.997 meters high, with a diameter of 1.68 meters and a total weight of 7 tons including the base. The inner side of the *ding* cauldron is inscribed with the characters meaning "The *ding* is made for celebration of Hong Kong's return to its motherland". The base of the *ding* is divided into two tiers: upper and lower. The upper base is 0.71m high, i.e. the specific date of Hong Kong's return to the motherland—July 1. It is octagonal in shape and decorated with 56 pieces of bronze dragon scales, symbolizing the return of Hong Kong to the motherland family consisting of 56 ethnic groups. The Chinses name of the *ding* is cast on the front of the upper base: Hong Kong Bao Ding. On the back were the producer's name and time of production. The

香港宝鼎
Hong Kong Bao Ding Cauldron

港,平稳发展,普天同庆,国运昌盛,安定繁荣。香港回归宝鼎象征总结香港过去、发展香港今天、开创香港未来。

2007年8月8日,在内蒙古自治区成立60周年之际,中央人民政府赠送给内蒙古自治区民族团结宝鼎。鼎身和鼎颈分别装饰着象征内蒙古山川地貌特点和牛羊成群景象的精美花纹。形如马鞍的鼎耳和形似马蹄的鼎足既象征蒙古族善于赛马射箭,又寓意吉祥如意、幸福安康。宝鼎是自治区政府所享有的民族自治权利和中华民族大团结的象征。

other six sides are carved with Chinese characters: One country, Two systems; the people of Hong Kong governing Hong Kong; Smooth Development; Universal Celebration; National Prosperity; Stability and Prosperity. The Hong Kong Bao Ding cauldron symbolizes the summing up of Hong Kong's past, the development of Hong Kong today, and the creation of Hong Kong's future.

内蒙古自治区的民族团结宝鼎
National Unity Ding in the Inner Mongolia Autonomous Region

On August 8, 2007, on the 60th anniversary of the founding of the Inner Mongolia Autonomous Region, the Central People's Government presented the autonomous region with the National Unity Ding. The body and neck of the *ding* were decorated with beautiful patterns symbolizing the characteristics of Inner Mongolia's mountains, rivers, and the sight of cattle and sheep flocks. The ears of the *ding*, in the shape of a saddle, and the foot of the *ding*, like a horse's hoof, symbolize the Mongolian people's skill in horse racing and archery, as well as their good fortune and happiness. The *ding* cauldron is a symbol of the autonomous power of the regional government and the great unity of the whole Chinese nation.

结 语

　　中原博大精深的青铜文明，尽情表达了华夏文化中对于自然的崇敬，对于上苍的信仰，对于生存繁衍的渴望，对于吉祥福瑞的向往，为后人留下了丰富的历史文化资源，这是人类共同的文化财富、精神源泉。这些集精美的造型与神奇的人文思想于一体的青铜器，融入了中国古代社会政治理念、文化思想、伦理道德、宗教意识和社会生活的各个方面，彰显了中华文化独一无二的理念、智慧、气度、神韵，承载着中华民族特有的人文追求和精神气质，在中华文明的传承中起到了重要作用。青铜文化对动物题材的偏爱反映了中原王朝文化的一种基本观念，即《易经·系辞上》中的"法象莫大乎天地"，是回归本真的表达和对天人合一境界的追求。人们在器物上铭刻族氏标记、家族荣耀、历史事件、道德告诫，以求后人"永宝用之"，表达了中国传统的价值观念。而青铜器精湛工艺背后的融合、创新，体现出中华民族的智慧和活力。经世代薪火相传的青铜文化，已深深植根于我们的传统文化之中，成为中华民族不断向前发展的精神纽带和内在动力。

Conclusion

The vast and profound bronze civilization of the Central Plains has expressed to the fullest extent the reverence for nature, the faith in Heaven, the wish for survival and reproduction, and the yearning for good fortune in Chinese culture, leaving behind a rich historical and cultural resource for future generations and is a cultural and spiritual source of mankind. These bronze objects, which unify exquisite shapes and magical humanistic ideas, incorporate the political philosophy, cultural thought, ethics, morality, religious consciousness, and all aspects of social life of ancient Chinese society, manifesting the unique concept, wisdom, temperament, and divinity of Chinese culture. They carry the unique humanistic pursuit and spirituality of the Chinese nation, and play an important role in the transmission of Chinese civilization. The preference for animal motifs in bronze culture reflects a basic concept of the culture of the Central Plains, namely, "the law and the image are as great as heaven and earth" as stated in the *Book of Changes*, which is an expression of the return to the true nature and the pursuit of the realm of unity between heaven and man. The inscriptions of clan marks, family glory, historical events, and moral admonitions on objects for future generations to "treasure forever" express the traditional Chinese value. The fusion and innovation behind the exquisite craftsmanship of the bronze objects reflects the wisdom and vitality of the Chinese nation. The bronze culture, which has been passed down through generations, is deeply rooted in our traditional culture and has become the spiritual bond and internal motivation for the continuous development of the Chinese nation.

附录：中国历史年代简表

Appendix: A Brief Chronology of Chinese History

中国历史年代简表
A Brief Chronology of Chinese History

五帝时代 Period of the Five Legendary Rulers c. 2600 BC–c. 2070 BC	黄帝 Huangdi (Yellow Emperor)	
	颛顼 Zhuanxu	
	帝喾 Diku (Emperor Ku)	
	尧 Yao	
	舜 Shun	
夏 Xia Dynasty	c. 2070 BC–c. 1600 BC	
商 Shang Dynasty	c. 1600 BC–c. 1046 BC	
西周 Western Zhou Dynasty	c. 1046 BC–c. 771 BC	
东周 Eastern Zhou Dynasty 770 BC–256 BC	春秋 Spring and Autumn Period	770 BC–476 BC
	战国 Warring States Period	475 BC–221 BC
秦 Qin Dynasty	221 BC–206 BC	
汉 Han Dynasty 206 BC–220 AD	西汉 Western Han	206 BC–25 AD
	东汉 Eastern Han	25 AD–220 AD
三国 Three Kingdoms 220 AD–280 AD	魏 Wei	220 AD–265 AD
	蜀汉 Shu Han	221 AD–263 AD
	吴 Wu	222 AD–280 AD
晋 Jin Dynasty 265 AD–420 AD	西晋 Western Jin	265 AD–317 AD
	东晋 Eastern Jin	317 AD–420 AD

续表 Continued Table

南北朝 Southern and Northern Dynasties 420 AD-589 AD	南朝 Southern Dynasties	宋 Song	420 AD-479 AD
		齐 Qi	479 AD-502 AD
		梁 Liang	502 AD-557 AD
		陈 Chen	557 AD-589 AD
	北朝 Northern Dynasties	北魏 Northern Wei	386 AD-534 AD
		东魏 Eastern Wei	534 AD-550 AD
		北齐 Northern Qi	550 AD-577 AD
		西魏 Western Wei	535 AD-556 AD
		北周 Northern Zhou	557 AD-581 AD
隋 Sui Dynasty		581 AD-618 AD	
唐 Tang Dynasty		618 AD-907 AD	
五代十国 Five Dynasties and Ten States	五代 Five Dynasties 907 AD-960 AD	后梁 Later Liang	907 AD-923 AD
		后唐 Later Tang	923 AD-936 AD
		后晋 Later Jin	936 AD-947 AD
		后汉 Later Han	947 AD-950 AD
		后周 Later Zhou	951 AD-960 AD
	十国 Ten States 902 AD-979 AD	北汉 Northern Han	951 AD-979 AD
		吴 Wu	902 AD-937 AD
		吴越 Wuyue	907 AD-978 AD
		闽 Min	909 AD-945 AD
		南汉 Southern Han	917 AD-971 AD
		荆南(又称"南平") Jingnan (Nanping)	924 AD-963 AD
		楚 Chu	927 AD-951 AD
		南唐 Southern Tang	937 AD-975 AD
		前蜀 Former Shu	907 AD-925 AD
		后蜀 Later Shu	934 AD-965 AD

续表 Continued Table

宋 Song Dynasty 960 AD-1279 AD	北宋 Northern Song	960 AD-1127 AD
	南宋 Southern Song	1127 AD-1279 AD
辽 Liao (契丹 Qidan/Khitan)	907 AD-1125 AD	
西夏 Xixia (Tangut)	1038 AD-1227 AD	
金 Jin	1115 AD-1234 AD	
元 Yuan Dynasty	1206 AD-1368 AD	
明 Ming Dynasty	1368 AD-1644 AD	
清 Qing Dynasty	1616 AD-1911 AD	
中华民国 Republic of China	1912 AD-1949 AD	
中华人民共和国 People's Republic of China	1949 AD-	